RAILWAY ~ MEMORIES

BARNSLEY
and Beyond

Peter Hadfield

A J11 0-6-0 and a Stanier Black 5 double head a holiday train in the 1950s through Summer Lane station after tackling the 1/69 gradient through the deep cutting around the Huddersfield Road and Victoria Road section of the line from Barnsley.

First published in Great Britain in 2015 by
Pen & Sword Transport
An imprint of Pen & Sword Books Ltd
47 Church Street
Barnsley
South Yorkshire
S70 2AS

Copyright © Peter Hadfield, 2015

ISBN 978 1 47385 648 6

The right of Peter Hadfield to be identified as the author of this
work has been asserted by him in accordance with the Copyright,
Designs and Patents Act 1988. All rights reserved. No part of this
publication may be reproduced or transmitted in any form or by
any means, electronic or mechanical, including photocopy,
recording or any information storage and retrieval system,
without the prior written permission of the publisher, nor by way
of trade or otherwise shall it be lent, re-sold, hired out or
otherwise circulated without the publisher's prior consent in any
form of binding or cover other than that in which it is published
and without a similar condition including this condition being
imposed on the subsequent purchaser.

Typeset by Pen & Sword Books Ltd
Printed and bound by Replika Press Pvt. Ltd.

Pen & Sword Books Ltd incorporates the imprints of Pen & Sword
Archaeology, Atlas, Aviation, Battleground, Discovery, Family
History, History, Maritime, Military, Naval, Politics, Railways,
Select, Social History, Transport, True Crime, and Claymore Press,
Frontline Books, Leo Cooper, Praetorian Press, Remember When,
Seaforth Publishing and Wharncliffe.

For a complete list of Pen and Sword titles please contact
Pen and Sword Books Limited
47 Church Street, Barnsley, South Yorkshire, S70 2AS, England
E-mail: enquiries@pen-and-sword.co.uk
Website: www.pen-and-sword.co.uk

CONTENTS

INTRODUCTION

Peter Hadfield as a boy.

MANY EXCELLENT BOOKS have been published about the railways around Barnsley and the surrounding area. This book is not an attempt to emulate them, it is a collection of memories which, hopefully, will bring to mind and stir the memories of all of us who lived through an era that, sadly, has disappeared.

'Time has a way of taking with it the demands of yesterday, and leaving with us the requirements of today.' I do not know who quoted that saying but it is perfectly true.

Our Headmaster at Hunningley Junior School, Mr Burgin, would recall to us the passage of barges through the Dearne and Dove canal's Aldham Eight Lock system. It would take the major part of a day to go through the lock system. My memories at this time (1956-1960) were of abandoned canals, but a thriving railway system. Today, much of the canal system and railway system has disappeared.

However, attempts are being made to restore the Dearne and Dove canal Elsecar branch and extend the private railway (once used by royalty, i.e. Edward VII), from the Elsecar Heritage Centre to the Cortonwood shopping centre.

Peter Hadfield.

Acknowledgements

I am indebted to the following people who have given assistance and photographs in the preparation of this book. Gerald Darby, Clive Pickering, Frank Johnson, Alwyn Bostwick, Steven Rymer, Bob Hadfield, A. L. Brown, John Westwood, Denise Hill, John Davies, Arthur Clayton, Gillian Nixon, Alan Ripley, Albert Godfrey and Patricia Faulkner.

Historical references: *Regional History of the Railways of Great Britain Volume 8 West and South Yorkshire* by David Joy.

British steam motive power depots LMR and Eastern regions by Paul Bolger.

While every effort has been made to trace the copyright holders of featured illustrations, this has not always proved possible because of the antiquity of the images.

Front Cover photograph: Jubilee 4-6-0, 45562 *Alberta* in Barnsley station, 1966.

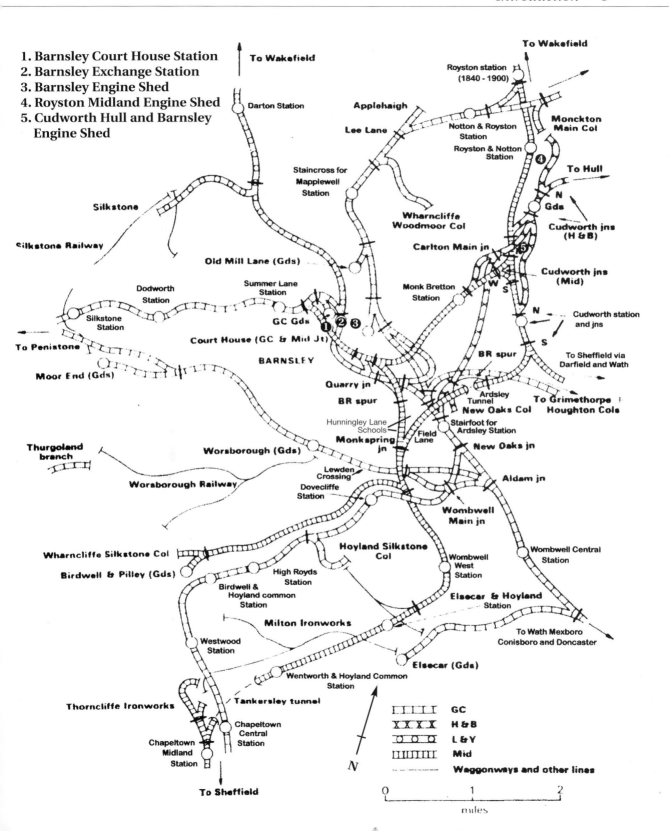

1. Barnsley Court House Station
2. Barnsley Exchange Station
3. Barnsley Engine Shed
4. Royston Midland Engine Shed
5. Cudworth Hull and Barnsley
   Engine Shed

Chapter One

FORMATIVE YEARS

WHERE DID MY passion for railways come from? Was it inherited from my mother, who had worked on the railway for the London Midland Scottish railway as a traffic controller at Cudworth Station during and after the 1939-45 Second World War? She loved the job and would often recall the memories etched in her mind. She remembered the LMS numbering of locomotives, i.e. four numbers, and an occasion when a prisoner of war train passing through the Cudworth sector was halted, following the escape of a number of PoWs. All rail traffic was stopped until their recapture.

My mother with fellow workers at Cudworth station during the late 1940s. *P. Hadfield*

One of my first recollections was viewing trains on the Barnsley to Sheffield line, which passed by Hunningley Lane infant school. The school can be seen to the right of the photograph. The picture shows Stanier Black 5 4-6-0 number 44693 heading the Halifax – St Pancras train near Hunningley Lane, 24 March 1962. *P. Hadfield*

My cousin, Terry, informs me that as a young boy he would take me down to Cudworth railway bridges, trainspotting. I cannot recall these early times but have no reason whatsoever to doubt him, as he looked after me like a brother. My first clear memories of my interest in trains was whilst I attended Hunningley Lane Infant School around 1955/56. My classroom had a view of the Barnsley to Sheffield line, (which opened in 1897), with the Barnsley to Sheffield passenger pull and push service being propelled by

Hunningley Lane Infants School shortly after closure in 1986. *P. Hadfield*

Stanier and Ivatt's 2-6-4 tanks 40148, 40181, 41274, 41281, 41282, operating out of the Royston, Leeds and Low Moor depots. All through spring, summer and autumn, before the dark nights crept in, (imagine this with

Field Lane bridge where I used to train spot particularly to watch the Thames-Clyde express Glasgow St Enoch to London St Pancras (during school holidays and Saturdays) and the 6pm London St Pancras – Bradford express along with freights and excursion specials. *A . Godfrey*

the concerns of parents today) – I would be allowed to go down Field Lane to watch the 6pm London St Pancras to Bradford express pass by. More often than not it would be a 4-6-0 Jubilee class engine hauling the train.

My first recollection of spotting Jubilees was at Swaithe Bridge, with my friend John Taylor. There we saw 45612 *Jamaica* and 45675 *Hardy*. Swaithe Bridge is situated on White Cross Lane, approximately 200-300 yards south of Monkspring Junction. The bridge at Field Lane, and the double signals

Jubilee class

The Jubilee Class of engines were introduced by Sir William Stanier in 1934. The Jubilees had a 4-6-0 wheel arrangement with taper boilers. All the locomotives were named predominantly after former British Commonwealth countries and states, British Admirals, Naval battles and ships. The class was built to haul express passenger and freight trains. There was a total of 191 in the class numbering from 45552 to 45742.

Four engines are still preserved today: 45593 *Kolhapur*, 45596 *Bahamas*, 45690 *Leander* and 45699 *Galatea*.

45562 *Alberta* photographed at Newcastle station with the Royal train in 1967. This locomotive is shown on the front cover at Barnsley Exchange station.

Royal Scot Class

The Royal Scot Class of engines were introduced in 1927 and then rebuilt in 1943 by Sir William Stanier with taper boilers, new cylinders and double chimneys. 46170 named *British Legion* was a rebuild of the high pressure compound locomotive No 6399 *Fury* (introduced 1929). British Railway's numbering was 46100 to 46170, a total of 71 in the class. They were predominantly named after British army regiments and were used to haul express passenger trains over the London Midland and Scottish region. Two engines are preserved today, 46100 *Royal Scot* and 46115 *Scots Guardsman*.

This photograph shows 6115 *Scots Guardsman* in LMS colours being renumbered 46115 in British Railway days along with green livery.

which were situated approximately 200-300 yards in the direction of Monkspring Junction, played an important part in my boyhood memories. We called it the Field Lane line, though its official name was the Chapeltown Loop. It was an alternative route to Sheffield. The main Midland mainline ran through Cudworth, Darfield, Wath-upon-Dearne joining the Sheffield to York line (originally known as the Swinton and Knottingley line) at Wath Road Junction, heading to Rotherham, through Rotherham Masborough Station, Meadowhall and finally into Sheffield. The Chapeltown Loop line (which came into use in 1899) branched off the main Midland line (which had opened to traffic in 1840, and was the first railway to come into the Barnsley area) south of Cudworth station and climbed towards Ardsley, crossed Sunny Bank viaduct at Lundwood, and

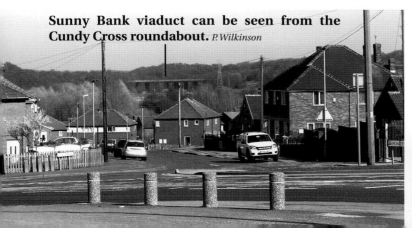

Sunny Bank viaduct can be seen from the Cundy Cross roundabout. *P. Wilkinson*

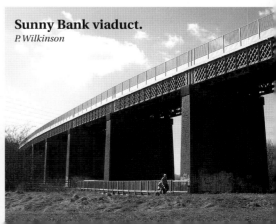

Sunny Bank viaduct.
P. Wilkinson

Hunningley Lane Junior School in 2015. The railway line runs to the left of the photograph. *P. Wilkinson*

then through Ardsley Tunnel, bridging the former LNER Great Central lines, via a large brick viaduct over Stairfoot, and over the Dearne and Dove Canal, Field Lane and finally at Monkspring Junction it joined the Barnsley to Sheffield line over Swaithe viaduct. The Wath to Penistone electrified line ran underneath, and the line was then bridged by the former Great Central Barnsley to Sheffield line which originally opened in 1854. It then climbed to Wombwell West station, then onto Elsecar, Wentworth for Hoyland Common, Chapeltown, Ecclesfield, Brightside, Attercliffe Road and finally into Sheffield Midland station.

The Chapeltown Loop line was built to ease traffic congestion at Wath and Rotherham, and was used as a diversionary route, although the line

North portal of the Ardsley tunnel as it looks today. *P. Wilkinson*

had booked trains running on it, i.e. the up Thames-Clyde and London St Pancras to Bradford expresses and many freights and excursion traffic.

The Field Lane line and nearby Stairfoot station were to play a major part in my boyhood love of the railways. I lived at 3 Ash Grove, Park House Estate, Kendray, and attended Hunningley Lane Junior School. This gave me and my pals, Norman Gill, Michael Watkin, John Lunn and Alan Ogley, to name a few, a unique opportunity to maintain our heady interest in the local railway scene. The school, as it is today, is situated adjacent to the Barnsley to Sheffield line.

Chapeltown loop lone trackbed Southern entrance to Ardsley Tunnel as it looked in1968. This entrance has been filled in and is no longer visible. *P. Hadfield*

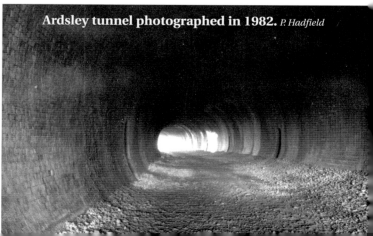

Ardsley tunnel photographed in 1982. *P. Hadfield*

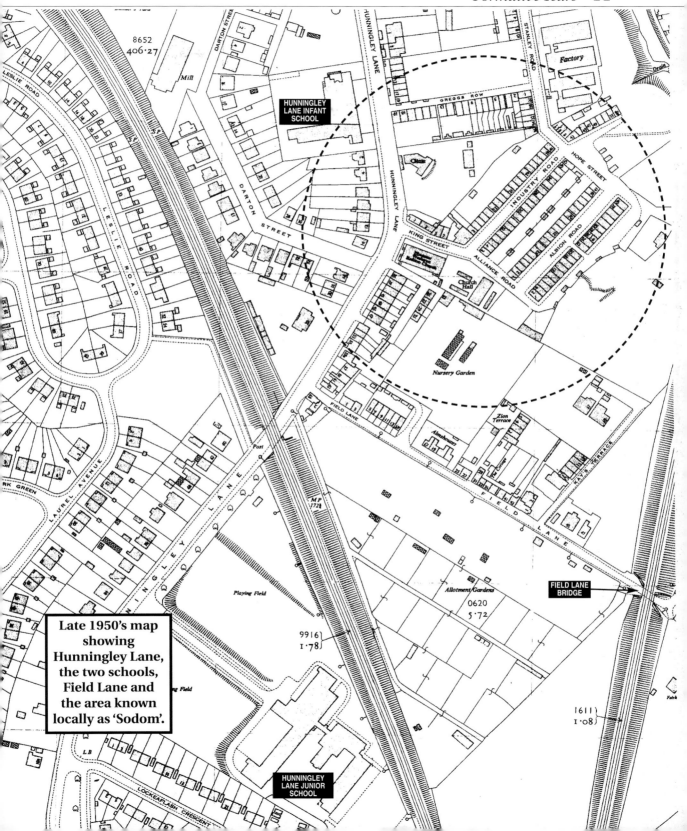

Late 1950's map showing Hunningley Lane, the two schools, Field Lane and the area known locally as 'Sodom'.

Britannia Class

4-6-2, 70013 *Oliver Cromwell.*

Following the nationalisation of the railways in 1948, further construction of steam locomotives was agreed to be of standard design, using the best features of the former four railway company's locomotives, i.e. London Midland Scottish Railway (LMS), London North Eastern Railway (LNER), Great Western Railway (GWR) and the Southern Railway (SR). The Britannia class introduced in 1951 was a product of this policy and a total of 55 were built. They were used for express passenger and freight work, operating over the entire railway system. British Railways numbers were 70000 to 70054, all named, with the exception of 70047. They were named after poets, soldiers, stars of the solar system, historical figures, writers, designers, army regiments and Scottish Firths.

Two engines have been preserved, 70000 *Britannia* and 70013 *Oliver Cromwell.*

Depending on which classroom you were in for your year, the Field Lane line was within easy viewing distance of the passing trains and their engine numbers. Stairfoot station and the surrounding sidings could also be seen in the distance.

Our teacher in classes 3A and 4A was Mrs Lewis, a woman of small stature, but with a commanding voice and hand when she felt punishment was required. She was a strict disciplinarian who did not tolerate any nonsense, but she was always willing to give praise when it was deserved. She was a good teacher and she recognised the futility of trying to gain our attention at around 3.20pm when the Thames – Clyde (Glasgow St Enoch to London St Pancras) express pounded up the gradient along the Field Lane line towards Monkspring Junction, before joining the Barnsley to Sheffield line. She would stop the lesson and allow the class to view the train. The engine and coaches were usually in good, clean condition and one of us would be sent outside to get the engine number. More often than not it would be a Leeds Holbeck shedded Jubilee or, occasionally, a Royal Scot or Britannia, then it would be back to the lesson.

Hours would be spent at Field Lane bridge, the double signals in the adjoining turnip field, known affectionately as the tup field. Originally this had been a cricket field and the roller used for the wicket was still there. Placing pennies on the line in the hope that the next train would make them the size of a half a crown was another activity undertaken. We had the advantage of spotting engines that came along the Barnsley to

View of the canal looking towards Stairfoot. The houses in the background were Albion Road, Hope Street, and Industry Road. These were in the area known as 'Sodom'. The Chapeltown loop line viaduct is shown with the engine in LMS lettering and guardsvan heading towards Field Lane and Monkspring Junction.

Sheffield line, the Field Lane line and of traffic that came through Stairfoot station. During a lull in rail traffic we would play on a raft on the disused canal. The raft comprised of a wooden frame from the gable end of houses that were being demolished in the area, or alternatively we would place wooden planks across the canal to walk across.

Adjacent to the Field Lane line and Hunningley Lane was a conurbation of terraced houses which had been built by Cammel-Laird, the shipbuilders based in Birkenhead, for the miners working at New Oaks Colliery. The mined coal was used as the fuel to raise steam in the days of steam powered ships. The New Oaks Colliery site was later occupied by the Yorkshire Tar Distillers works which was situated off Wombwell Lane.

Albion Road, Industry Road, Greggs Row and Stanley Road were four of the streets that spring to mind that made up the area affectionately known as 'Sodom'. This was a close knit community which, comprised of a

Back of Greggs Row and Stanley Road.

majority of good, decent people, and a very small number who were not regarded as such. It was in your own interests to be known in the neighbourhood and not fall foul of the undesirable element, who were known to even turn on their own. My friend, Dennis Taylor, and I fell foul of this faction and on one occasion found ourselves in the canal, along with our bicycles. Despite this we spent many happy times in the area and although this book is dedicated to railway memories it is, I feel, worthwhile relating the story of the day in between trainspotting, running along a plank, placed across the canal on the banks, back and forth. One of our school friends, Brian Starkie, who had earlier in his life suffered burns to his body, lost his balance on the plank and fell into the canal. Covered in green algae and thoroughly wet through, we accompanied him to his home on Greggs Row. We had on that day brought a dog with us called Monty, a 'Heinz 57' variety, belonging to the Skidmore family who lived near to our homes. 'Monty' would follow us wherever we went.

When we reached Brian's home he received the customary 'telling off' from his mother and then went upstairs to get a change of clothing. We were stood in the doorway of his home, along with our four-legged friend when Brian's father appeared, probably after a customary session in

Stairfoot's beer hostelries, not totally drunk, but not experiencing 20-20 vision. Brian's mother had cooked a joint of meat from which Brian's father was going to carve a piece of meat to make a sandwich, before departing to the 'land of nod' as part of his preparation to be of sound body and mind for the night session. He proceeded to then carve a piece of meat from the joint for the dog, which he left on the same plate as the joint and offered it to the dog. He must have assumed that Monty would understand that his was the small piece. Monty, quite naturally, went for the larger piece which seemed to be on offer and he grabbed the whole joint in his jaws and made a hasty exit from the house. Brian's father stood there amazed but Brian's mother was far from impressed and when Brian appeared downstairs, he was hastily sent back upstairs with a clip around the ear. My friend and I realised that this fate may befall us, so we made a hasty departure from the house, amid the shouts of 'stop that dog' or words to that effect. Fellow residents chased Monty in Keystone Cops fashion, but to no avail. As we reached home, Monty was just starting to enjoy the bone from the joint, as the meat had long gone into his stomach.

The predominant traffic through Stairfoot was of a freight nature with Barnsley and Mexborough sheds' O1s, O2s, O4s, J11s and 9Fs providing the motive power, along with Royston's 4Fs, 8Fs and 9Fs.

A newspaper train would pass through Stairfoot in the early hours of the morning, coming from Manchester. I was never allowed, and rightly so, to go to Stairfoot at that time of the morning, but I understand that motive power could be in the form of a B1, V2, K3 and, on occasions, a Pacific (i.e. A1, A2 or A3).

A fish train from the east coast would pass through Stairfoot in the early evening, usually a B1 providing the motive power and an occasional named engine, e.g. 61247 *Lord Burghley* and 61379 *Mayflower*.

B1 4-6-0, 61247 *Lord Burghley* **of Doncaster shed photographed in 1953.** *P. Hadfield*

The RCTS rail tour pauses at Stairfoot station on 21 September 1958. The lead engine is B1 4-6-0, 61165. The 2nd engine is the now preserved ex-Great Central Director D11 class 4-4-0, 62660 *Butler Henderson*. The view is looking towards Aldham and Wombwell with the Yorkshire Tar Distillers, Stairfoot works, in the background. The terminus of the Hull and Barnsley freightline can be seen directly below the signal box.

Chapter Two

STAIRFOOT STATION

STAIRFOOT, IN PARTICULAR the station, was where I spent many happy hours. The station was originally called Ardsley, but was renamed Stairfoot for Ardsley, to avoid confusion with the Ardsley near Wakefield. The original station was situated along Wombwell Lane, across from the row of terraced houses still standing today, which was known as Deputy Row. The station was the scene of a tragic accident on 12 December 1870, when ten wagons got free during shunting operations in

Looking towards Stairfoot brickworks. On the right is Wombwell Lane where the same houses stand today. They were originally known as Deputy Row. The original Stairfoot station was across from these houses. *P. Hadfield*

Barnsley, and careered down the gradient to Stairfoot, crashing into the rear of a stationary Barnsley to Sheffield train in the station. Fourteen people were killed and fifty injured. The nearby *Cross Keys* public house (now demolished) was used as a mortuary.

Miners connected with the Oaks Colliery were holding a meeting at *The Cross Keys* when the accident occurred. It was on that very day four years earlier that the Oaks Colliery disaster took place. When the men heard a loud crash they rushed to the station to help rescue the victims. The station was in total darkness until fires from the wreckage lit up the tragic scene. Gradually the dead and wounded were lifted out and placed on the station platform, they were then carried to the adjoining houses and to *The Cross Keys* and *Keel Inn*.

Photo courtesy of Michael Chance, Ardsley & Stairfoot Revisited

APPALLING
RAILWAY DISASTE[R]
NEAR BARNSLEY.

FOURTEEN PERSONS KILLED
AND MANY INUJRED.

R E V I S E D
LIST OF KILLED AND WOUNDED

DETAILED ACCOUNT
OF

THE SCENE OF THE COLLISION,
THE COLLISION,
THE RECOVERY OF THE DEAD AND DYING,
CLEARING THE LINE, CAUSE OF
THE ACCIDENT.

THE EXCITEMENT IN THE DISTRICT.
LETTER FROM A PASSENGER.

T H E   I N Q U E S T.
VERDICT OF MANSLAUGHTER.
INCIDENTS, NARROW ESCAPES, &c.

The twelfth of December is a fatal day in the annals of Barnsley and neighbourhood. Four years ago, on that day, occurred the dreadful and never to be forgotten explosion at the Oaks Colliery which, with subsequent disasters, proved fatal to 361 individuals. On the morning of the same day, three years ago, the inhabitants of the district were shocked with the announcement of the sanguinary conflict which resulted in the death of George Thirkill, late head keeper to Lord Wharncliffe.

Stairfoot station 1912/13 looking towards Barnsley.

A new station was built and opened on 1 December 1871. This was the location where I spent many happy hours. The station closed to passenger traffic on 16 September 1957. It has long since been demolished and the site is now occupied by McDonalds. My earliest memory was being allowed by the stationmaster to light the platform lights, which were still operated by gas, not electricity; I remember the 'F' on the 'Stairfoot for Ardsley' station sign on one of the platforms was hanging off. My neighbours at home, Mr Bill Cousins and Mr Bill Nutton who were driver and fireman, respectively, were based at Barnsley shed. They stopped at Stairfoot station with a freight train, and invited me onto the footplate of the engine. For a young boy this was a tremendous experience.

There are many memories etched in my mind of times spent on the station. I remember arriving at the station one morning with one of my friends, Ian Caldwell, and seeing B1s 61247 *Lord Burghley* and 61250 *A Harold Bibby* – a rare sight to see two named engines in the station at the same time.

B1 4-6-0, 61250 *A Harold Bibby* in Doncaster shed. This engine regularly pulled the Penistone – Barnsley – Doncaster train.
P. Hadfield

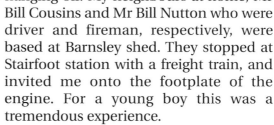

Stairfoot station photographed in the 1950s. *P. Hadfield*

The Pennine Pullman heads through Stairfoot station on the 12 May 1956, pulled by ex Great Central Directors D11 class 4-4-0s, 62664 *Princess Mary* and 62662 *Prince of Wales*. The Chapeltown loop line viaduct bridge is in the background. Notice the 'f' on the station sign is hanging off.

Stairfoot station was behind where McDonalds stands on this present day photograph. *P. Wilkinson*

Another occasion is when B1 61001 *Eland* came into the station, light engine. On that day I was on my own, and convincing my fellow trainspotter friends back home that this locomotive had visited Stairfoot was not easy. To mark an engine down in your spotter's book without seeing it (known as cabbaging) was considered to be sacrilege.

I would spend the day on the station, dreaming of going to Doncaster, seeing the locomotives shown in the spotter's book, i.e. A4s streaks, e.g. *Mallard*; A3s, e.g. *Flying Scotsman*; A2s, e.g. *Blue Peter*; A1s, e.g. *Meg Merrilies*; V2s, e.g. *Green Arrow*; B1s; B16/17s; Sandringhams (Sandies), e.g. *Barnsley*.

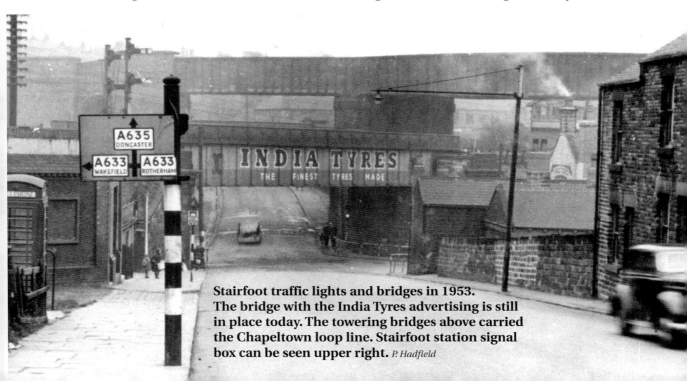

Stairfoot traffic lights and bridges in 1953. The bridge with the India Tyres advertising is still in place today. The towering bridges above carried the Chapeltown loop line. Stairfoot station signal box can be seen upper right. *P. Hadfield*

The RCTS. 'South Yorkshireman' Railtour, viewed from the footbridge of Stairfoot for Ardsley railway station on 21 September, 1958. The lead engine was B1 4-6-0, 61165 and the second engine preserved Director D11 4-4-0, 62660 *Butler Henderson*. *P. Hadfield*

The advantage of spotting on Stairfoot station was that you could note the engines going through the station and the engines traversing the Chapeltown Loop via the viaduct over Stairfoot.

The majority of engines passing through the station were freight, mainly carrying coal to and from Wath marshalling yard, sidings at Barnsley Main, Mitchell Main, Wombwell Main collieries, Yorkshire Tar Distillers, Stairfoot works. Royston sheds 4Fs, 8Fs and austerities would pass through the station, bringing freight and coal from Carlton Marshalling yards, using the Hull and Barnsley line, which found its route through Redfearn National Glass works (now Ardagh) at Monk Bretton, Lundwood (now part of the Trans-Pennine Trail), finally to Stairfoot, which was the terminus of the line. Cudworth was the passenger terminus.

The owners originally intended to extend further west, but were not

**An unidentified B1 4-6-0 named engine stopping in Stairfoot station with a
passenger train, awaiting right of way signals before continuing to Barnsley.**
P. Hadfield

successful. Stairfoot, in the heyday of the railways, was a place where
passengers could go to Doncaster, Sheffield, Leeds and Barnsley, with
subsequent connections to the major cities of the UK. By the time I was
spotting on the station (i.e. mid-1950s and onward), most of the services
had been severely curtailed. The Penistone to Barnsley Court House to
Doncaster service was the predominant one. The Barnsley to Sheffield
Victoria service had terminated in 1953, before my time at the station. The
service to Doncaster, as I remember, comprised of trains departing
Stairfoot at approximately 8.10am and 10.00am, with the returning train at
6.00pm. I cannot recall seeing Barnsley shed's J11s (Pom-Poms) C13s, and
C14s being used on the service as they certainly were, along with the
occasional ex-GCR D11 Director. Mexborough shed's B1s were
predominantly used, e.g. 61165, 61166, 61167, Doncaster shed's 61250 *A*

Class J11 0-6-0, 64366 and a B1 class engine double head a passenger train out of Stairfoot toward Barnsley in the 1950s. The train was probably a working men's club trip or a holiday excursion to the coast. *P. Hadfield*

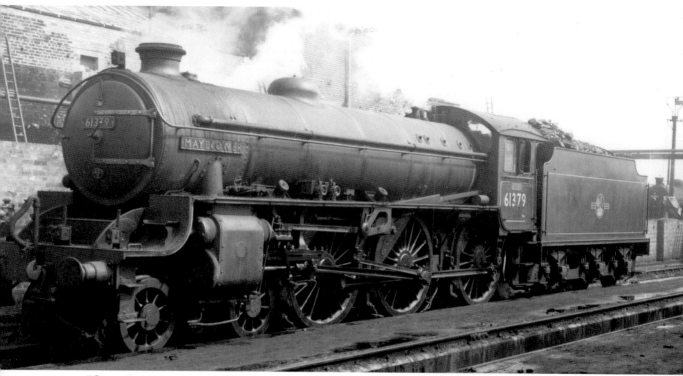

There is a preserved B1 4-6-0, 61306 which carries the name *Mayflower* but 61379, as shown in the above photograph, was the original engine named *Mayflower*.

Harold Bibby, 61266 and Immingham sheds' 61379 *Mayflower*.

During the summer, specials would pass through to the holiday resorts and Belle Vue Zoo, Manchester. Many specials would stop at the station to pick up passengers. Working men's club day trips to the coast would pass through. Ashfield WMC's club trip used the station, usually going to Cleethorpes, Bridlington or Scarborough for the day. On one of the Ashfield WMC trips to Cleethorpes, I remember arriving at Cleethorpes and Britannia class 4-6-2, 70009 *Alfred the Great* was in the station.

Freight and coal traffic used the Barnsley Coal Railway. Its route was from Wakefield through Ryhill, Notton, Royston, Staincross (of which the stationmaster's house still stands and is occupied). Through New Lodge, Smithies, sidings to Old Mill Goods, Mottram Wood Colliery, Hoyle Mill (now the Dearne Valley Park), siding to Wood Brothers Glass and Barnsley Brewery. It also served local collieries, for example, Wharncliffe Woodmoor, 1, 2 and 3 units and finally to Stairfoot station. Occasionally diverted passenger traffic would also use the line. The line had not seen regular passenger traffic since the Barnsley to Leeds service had

Brush type 2 D5819 heading towards Stairfoot on the Barnsley coal railway with coal wagons. The bridge and houses in the background are still present today at the junction of Wakefield road and Burton road. Wickes DIY store now stands on this site today. *P. Hadfield*

terminated in 1930. The Coal Railway had stations at Staincross, Royston/Notton and Ryhill (Ryhill had the benefit of two stations, the other being on the Dearne Valley line at Cow Lane. The Coal Railway ran through Wintersett to join the LNER line near Walton).

This service was an alternative to the Barnsley to Leeds service that is

B1 class 4-6-0, 61165 of Mexborough shed leaving Stairfoot station with the Penistone-Barnsley-Doncaster train towards Wombwell in the 1950s. Yorkshire Tar Distillers works can be seen in the background. *P. Hadfield*

New Oaks Junction, Stairfoot, 18 July 1967. Royston sheds' 8F's 2-8-0s 48473 Wath yard to Carlton and 48113 leaving Stairfoot with a Carlton to Wath yard train. New Oaks signal box and Yorkshsire Brick Company, Stairfoot works, can be seen in the background. *P. Hadfield*

used today, through Darton, Crigglestone, Wakefield Kirkgate and onwards to Leeds. A pilot engine would be on standby in the siding adjacent to the station signal box, and was available to assist heavy coal trains on the incline up to Barnsley. On occasions, dependent on the engine crew and signalman, I would be allowed on the footplate and in the signal box. Freight traffic from Barnsley using the Barnsley Coal Railway would use (traverse) the Stairfoot curve, avoiding Stairfoot station. The curve encompassed the former Beatson Clark Glass works and joined the Coal Railway from Stairfoot at Hoyle Mill, with the towering Oaks viaduct above. Leaving Stairfoot along the Coal Railway, a single line left the Coal Railway at Stairfoot North Junction, bridging Grange Lane, under the Hull and Barnsley railway, running adjacent to Ardsley tunnel, and passing under the Chapeltown Loop line near to Sunny Bank viaduct. It then went through Horse Carr and Storrs Mill Woods, over the Midland main line section between Cudworth and Darfield, with the line splitting to serve Grimethorpe, Houghton Main and Dearne Valley collieries. In Horse Carr Wood a stream fed a water tank which would be used to replenish the engine's water supply.

Stairfoot 1951

1. Stairfoot/Ardsley station
2. *The Cross Keys*
3. Dearne and Dove Canal
4. Deputy Row houses on Wombwell Lane
5. *Keel Inn*
6. Area known as 'Sodom'
7. Yorkshshire Tar Distillers works
8. Tomlinson's Glass Works
9. Stairfoot Brickworks clay quarry
10. The *Black Bull Inn* which still stands today
11. Road to Cundy Cross
12. Road to Barnsley (Doncaster Road
13. To Ardsley
14. To Wombwell

1

BEATSON. CLARK & C? LT

Stairfoot 1951

1. Ardsley Tunnel
2. Road to Cundy Cross
3. Dearne and Dove Canal
4. Hoyle Mill Road - Oaks Lane

*View towards Barnsley
from Stairfoot 1951*

1. Beatson Clark glassworks
2. Barnsley Main colliery
3. Dearne and Dove Canal
4. Barnsley Main colliery
5. Oaks Viaduct
6. Barnsley Aquaduct
7. Burton Road
8. Rotherham Road to Cundy Cross

Chapter Three

SWAITHE AND DOVECLIFFE STATION

DURING THE SCHOOL holidays in the late fifties and early sixties, when life seemed so carefree, I, along with my friends John Lunn, Norman Gill, David Carroll, Ian Caldwell, Jimmy Oxley, Michael Watkin and Alan Ogley, would spend all day playing in the woods at Swaithe, affectionately known as 'Black Pad'. We would make a swing across the River Dove and climb the quarry face in Dovecliffe quarry. The electrified line at Swaithe (Black Pad) was part of the Woodhead (Sheffield to Manchester) electrification scheme, initially starting in the late 1930s, but curtailed by the Second World War. Work recommenced in the late 1940s, with the Wath to

Dovecliffe station as it looked in the early 1900s, looking towards Swaithe and Wombwell.

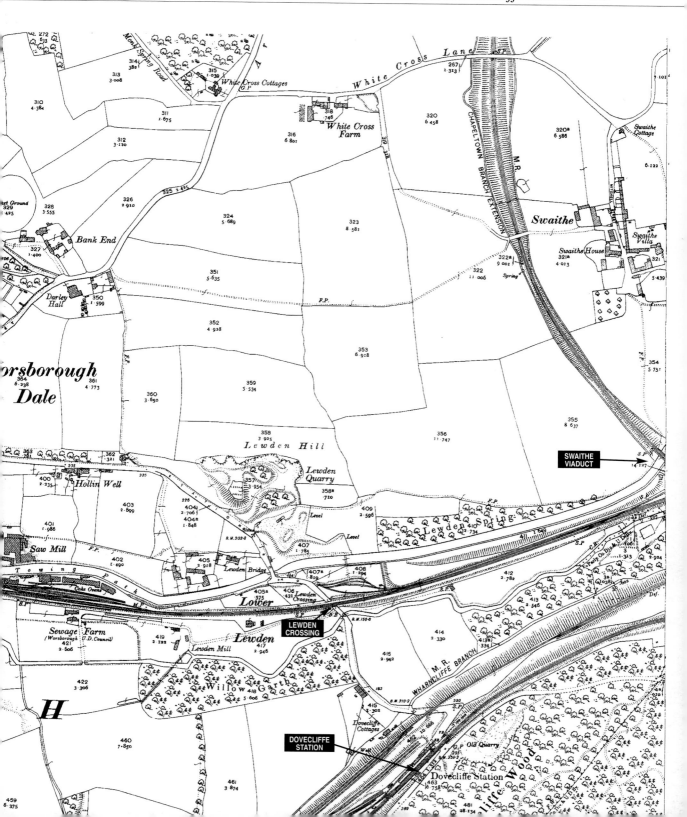

Dovecliffe station in 1953 with a Mexborough shed O4 2-8-0, 63751 heading empty coal wagons for refilling at either Barrow, Rockingham, or Wharncliffe Silkstone collieries.

Dovecliffe station as it looked in 1910, looking towards Barrow, Rockingham and Birdwell.

Penistone section being completed in 1952 and the full scheme (Sheffield to Manchester) being completed in 1954, incorporating the opening of the new Woodhead tunnel.

The main line was from Sheffield Victoria to Manchester London Road (now Piccadilly), with branches to Rotherwood and Wath. The Wath to Penistone section joined the Barnsley to Penistone line at West Silkstone Junction, before progressing to Penistone.

Prior to the opening of the Wath to Penistone section – completed from Moor End to West Silkstone Junction in 1880, – freight traffic from Wath would go through Barnsley, Summer Lane, Dodworth, Silkstone Common and Penistone, before traversing the Pennines to Manchester. Barnsley was heavily congested and, therefore, it was decided to connect the existing Aldham Junction (Wombwell) to Moor End section, by a further extension (as aforementioned) from Moor End to West Silkstone Junction, therefore avoiding Barnsley. The line was steeply graded, the most severe section being from Wentworth Junction to West Silkstone Junction, where a gradient of 1:38/40 was encountered. In steam days up to four

Dovecliffe station as it looked in 1980, looking towards Swaithe and Wombwell. Platform remains can be seen on the right. *P. Hadfield*

locomotives would be required to haul the heavy coal trains up to Penistone. In 1925 a Garratt type locomotive was constructed by LNER to bank the trains, particularly up the Wentworth Junction to West Silkstone Junction section. The Garratt was shedded at Mexborough but spent a large amount of time in a siding at Wentworth Junction awaiting banking duties. Working conditions for crews were horrendous, particularly passing through the two Silkstone tunnels, crews would have masks and would lay on the footplate to avoid being suffocated, speed at this point being no more than 4/5mph at a maximum. Therefore, the completion of the electrification scheme resulted in vastly improved working conditions for crews, and freight train times were speeded up.

Although my love of steam was foremost in my mind, I soon gained an affinity for the electric locomotives in their British Railways, green livery

The Garratt locomotive built in 1925 for assisting the coal/freight trains up the Worsborough Bank gradient in particularly the Wentworth Junction to the West Silkstone Junction section. *P. Hadfield*

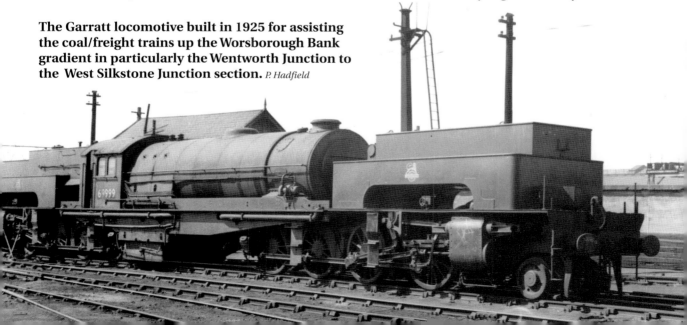

and some of the engines being named. The original locomotive (BR No 26000) had been built by the LNER in 1940, and worked on the Dutch railway after 1945. It was affectionately christened by the Dutch *Tommy* in appreciation of the British soldiers who liberated the Dutch from the Germans during the latter stages of the Second World War. Two classes of locomotives were constructed for working the Woodhead route, EM1s and EM2s. The EM1s (fifty eight in total) were predominantly used for freight, although they were used on the passenger service from Sheffield Victoria to Manchester London Road (Piccadilly). The building of the EM2s was curtailed, only seven being constructed which were specifically used on the passenger service. Some EM1s also had the benefit of being named (always a bonus for any trainspotter) after famous people of ancient Greece, e.g. *Archimedes, Diomedes, Hector, Jason, Perseus, Ulysses.* The EM2s were all named and carrying on the same theme, e.g. *Minerva, Aurora, Pandora.*

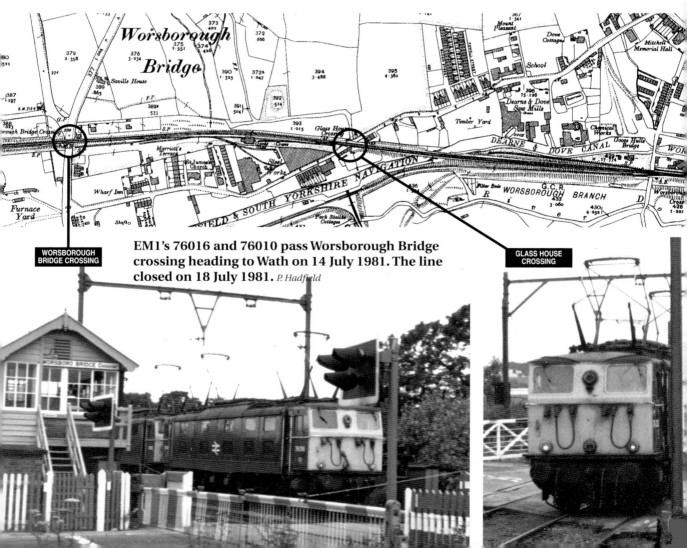

WORSBOROUGH
BRIDGE CROSSING

EM1's 76016 and 76010 pass Worsborough Bridge crossing heading to Wath on 14 July 1981. The line closed on 18 July 1981. *P. Hadfield*

GLASS HOUSE
CROSSING

The line through Dovecliffe was the original Barnsley to Sheffield line, coming to Barnsley in 1854. Dovecliffe was originally named Smithley for Darley Main and Worsbrough and Darkcliffe, before finally acquiring the Dovecliffe name. The line lost its passenger service on 7 December 1953, therefore, predominant freight traffic was coal from Barrow, Rockingham and Wharncliffe Silkstone collieries and coke from Barrow Coking Plant. Birdwell and Hoyland Common station, although closed after 7 December 1953, along with Dovecliffe, still received special passenger workings, e.g. Working Men's Club trips. The through route to Sheffield was severed by the construction of the M1 motorway at Birdwell during the mid/late 1960s.

Therefore, a day spent at Swaithe Dovecliffe and in Lewden crossing box gave the advantage of spotting engines going over Swaithe viaduct,

EM1s 76016 and 76010 leave Lewden crossing heading towards Aldham and Wombwell on 6 July 1981. Swaithe viaduct can be seen in the background. *P. Hadfield*

the electrics and steam freights through Dovecliffe station.

In between trainspotting we would climb the trees, as previously mentioned, and swing across the River Dove. This reminds me of an occasion of not picking my feet up high enough and trailing them in the river, leaving me stationary in the middle of the river, with no alternative but to drop. Fortunately, the river was shallow at this point and I was able to wade out. We would also play in what were, in our opinion, old coking or brick kilns on the site of the former Swaithe Main Colliery, which had been the scene of a tragic explosion in 1875, when 143 men and boys were killed.

The Barnsley to Sheffield line through Dovecliffe joined at Wombwell Main Junction, with a branch to Wombwell Main Colliery, serving the line, originally, trains had to reverse at Aldham Junction before continuing to Stairfoot and Barnsley. However, following the construction of the curve from Wombwell Main to New Oaks Junction, Stairfoot in 1879, trains could now run direct. A branch line from the Midland near Swaithe viaduct also served the

Notice of withdrawal of passenger services on the former Great Central Sheffield – Barnsley line, 7 December 1953. *P. Hadfield*

Birdwell and Hoyland Common station.

Barrow, Rockingham, Wharncliffe Silkstone collieries and coking plant complexes.

Before leaving the Field Lane, Stairfoot, Dovecliffe, Swaithe (Black Pad) area, the locomotives that spring to mind, seen on a regular basis, were Jubilees: *Nova Scotia, Saskatchewan, Alberta, New South Wales, Victoria, Queensland, Western Australia, Newfoundland, Gwailor, Travancore, Seychelles, Zanzibar, Raleigh, Shovell, Hood, Keyes, Kempenfelt, Hardy, Ulster*; and Royal Scots: *Royal Scot Fusilier, The York and Lancaster Regiment* and the *Duke of Wellington's Regiment* (West Riding). The rarer ones on the Thames to Clyde Express were Jubilee, *Leeward Islands*, double-headed with a Black Five, Britannia *Earl Haig*, the 7.15pm light

45048 *Royal Marines* at the Worsborough Bridge crossing, on its return to Wath in 1980. *P. Hadfield*

A MR 4-4-0 hauling an express over Swaithe viaduct in Midland days. The photograph is taken from the bank of the Worsborough Branch of the Dearne and Dove canal and looking towards Wombwell. The Wath to Penistone line, later to be electrified, is visible below. In the foreground, adjacent to the signal, is the siding line that lead to Swaithe Main Colliery. The Wath – Penistone line is no longer in existence, the track is removed and the trackbed forms part of the Trans Pennine Trail.
The viaduct and line is still in use today forming part of the Barnsley – Sheffield line

Similiar view in 2015.

View from the other side of the viaduct looking back towards Worsborough. The viaduct is undergoing repair work.

Arthur Clayton

EM1 26048 *Hector* leaving Swaithe and heading towards Wombwell Main, 1960.
A. Godfrey

View underneath the Swaithe viaduct in 1960 showing the electrified line underneath. *A. Godfrey*

engine Britannia *Moray Firth*, *Patriot*, *Duke of Sutherland* on a special working.

The memory of the latter sighting was of several of us, including Kevin Durkin, John Taylor (both sadly now not with us), Gary and Ian Caldwell and John Lunn, jumping for joy as the *Duke of Sutherland* was rarely seen in this area. Such was the euphoria and interest for boys that trainspotting held before the 'wine, women and song' years took over. Finally, EM1 26000 *Tommy* was also seen at Swaithe.

Patriot class 4-6-0, 45541
Duke of Sunderland.

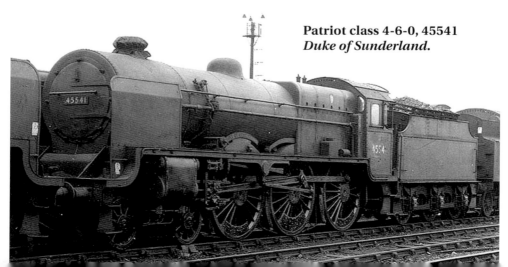

Chapter Four

CUDWORTH, CARLTON, ROYSTON AND THE OAKS VIADUCT

AS MENTIONED AT the beginning of this book, my mother had worked at Cudworth Station during and after the Second World War. The line was the first to reach the outskirts of Barnsley in 1840 and, indeed, the station was first named Barnsley before being renamed Cudworth in 1854. The line became the Midland Main line between Leeds and Sheffield, add the concentration yards at Carlton, the Hull and Barnsley yard and line, the Hull and Barnsley shed, Royston LMS shed, Cudworth and Royston's extensive stations, it was

The extensive railway station at Cudworth in Midland railway days, looking towards Storrs Mill and Darfield. The station has been demolished with no trace left, however the water tank building shown on left remains today.

L.S. 221-2. Midland Railway Station, Cudworth.

The building on the right is the former Hull and Barnsley station used later as the area control centre where my mother worked. Cudworth brickworks and chimney can be seen in the distance.

Another view of the former Hull and Barnsley station with the five platforms of the Midland on the left and the platform of the Hull and Barnsley on the right of the photograph. Making Cudworth an extensive station layout. A passenger train can be seen entering the station on the left

Another early view of the station in Midland days looking towards Carlton,

not hard to imagine that this area was a Mecca for trainspotters.

I did not venture much onto Cudworth station, I would spend time, on some occasions at Cudworth bridges, but more often than not at Carlton. My mother originated from Monk Bretton and her sister, my Auntie Frances and my Uncle Tom, lived originally in Newsome Square in the old village. After the village was demolished (regrettably, in my opinion) in the name of progress, they moved to 8 Orchard Close, Monk Bretton. I spent a fair amount of time during school holidays and weekends at my Auntie Frances and Uncle Tom's home and, whenever possible, I would make my way to the railway at Carlton. I would walk along Fish Dam Lane, Far Field Lane, sometimes on Carlton Long Row through Wharncliffe Woodmoor,

A 4F 0-6-0 trundles through the station with a freight train along platform three in 1953.

units 4, 5 and 6 colliery yard, and finally through a tunnel, nicknamed the 'monkey tunnel', emerging alongside the Midland Main line. I would spend the day being treated to an almost endless procession of trains – the famed trains such as *Thames Clyde Express*, *The Devonian*, *The Waverley*, Express goods, e.g. *The Condor*, usually engines and rolling stock in immaculate condition, alongside the Leeds to Sheffield local passenger

A special organised by the Stephenson locomotive and Midland locomotive societies routed from Manchester to Hull via the Hull and Barnsley railway, pauses in Cudworth in early British Railway days. Note the LMS lettering on the tender but the British railways number on the engine which is 2P 4-4-0, 40726 shedded at Canklow shed code 19c.

traffic, and finally, the numerous freight trains entering and leaving the Carlton and former Hull and Barnsley marshalling yards. This would be followed up by a visit to Royston's former LMS shed. The Hull and Barnsley shed had closed in 1951, before my excursions to the area.

Royston shed was a freight shed and locomotives allocated to the shed were mainly 4Fs, 8Fs and austerities but, on occasions, a visiting Jubilee or

Britannia could be seen. Royston shed was home to the tank engines used on the Barnsley to Sheffield and Cudworth to Barnsley pull and push services. I never had the opportunity to travel on the train, but I did see it on many occasions leaving Cudworth and passing alongside Monk Bretton Colliery where my Dad worked. He would take me during school holidays on a Friday to collect his weekly wage. I seem to recollect that the wages office was situated adjacent to the entrance of the site of Monk Bretton station, which had closed in 1937, the station buildings and platforms had been demolished.

The pull and push service would leave Cudworth station, take the Cudworth South Junction curve, passing the former Redfearn's Glass works (now Ardagh), bridging the Hull and Barnsley freight line to Stairfoot, passing the site of Monk Bretton Station and underneath Burton Road, Monk Bretton Colliery and sidings, underneath Littleworth Lane and

Rotherham Road, and then crossing the Dearne Valley at Hoyle Mill by means of the iconic 1,000ft long lattice structured Oaks Viaduct (sadly demolished in 1968). Then it went underneath Oaks Lane, followed the perimeter of Barnsley Main Colliery spoil heap, bridged Oakwell Lane, Pontefract Road, the Barnsley to Stairfoot former Great Central line at Jumble Lane by a viaduct which ran adjacent to Barnsley bus station and, finally, into the Barnsley Court House station. The service terminated in June 1958 and the line predominantly abandoned, but sections were still used to serve Monk Bretton and Barnsley Main collieries and Redfearn's Glass company, but the through route over Oaks Viaduct was severed. I did cross the viaduct, when it was abandoned, both when the disused rails were in and out of situ. With today's attitude towards preserving our heritage, it may be still standing, as is the viaduct at Sunny Bank. Just imagine what an impressive feature of the Dearne Valley Park the Oaks

A preserved 44932, 4-6-0 Black Five on route to Butterley passes through Cudworth, 1986. *G. Darby*

Preserved West Country Class 4-6-2, 34092 *City of Wells* passes through Cudworth 1 November 1985. *P. Hadfield*

Viaduct would have been.

Jubilee 4-6-0, 45662 *Kempenfelt* at Cudworth. The lane in the foreground led up to the station and is still there today. *A.Ripley*

Jubilee 4-6-0, 45573 *Newfoundland* in Cudworth station in 1949. The LMS lettering is still shown on the tender. *A.Ripley*

Jubilees 4-6-0s, 45607 *Fiji* **(above) and 45564** *New South Wales* **(opposite) at Cudworth in 1964. By this date many of the express passenger services were being hauled by diesels, in particular the Peak class. Withdrawals of the Jubilee class were taking place at an increasing rate, and the remaining were predominantly being relegated to secondary passenger, relief and freight services. The engines were not being maintained in good external condition as the photographs show.** *A. Ripley*

Jubilee 45564 *New South Wales* **at Cudworth, 1964.** *A. Ripley*

41273 on the pull-push Barnsley to Cudworth. Photographed at Cudworth station. *A. Ripley*

BR Standard 73046 at Cudworth. *P. Hadfield*

An 8F on freight passing through Cudworth, the lane to the left is one approach to the station the other being Station Road. *A. Ripley*

Class 47 47431 heads towards Darfield from Cudworth station in 1985.
P. Hadfield

Peak class 45105 passes Cudworth station in 1985.
P. Hadfield

HST *City of Peterborough* passes Cudworth towards Darfield in 1985. The remains of platform 1 buildings can be seen to the left. Track removal of the down main line has taken place, the up mainline track is still in place. *P. Hadfield*

A diesel hauled passenger train passes Carlton Marshalling yards in the 1960s.
P. Hadfield

The former Hull and Barnsley shed shortly before closure in 1951. The Carlton marshalling yards and Royston Midland shed can be seen in the distance.
P. Hadfield

The original Royston station was situated at old Royston from 1840 to 1900 and was replaced by the station shown below. The photograph shows the new Midland station which was situated off Midland Road with the entrance to the station being adjacent to the Royston Railways club (still open today) and the Station House (now a domestic residence). A freight line is still in use to deliver glass making materials to the Ardagh (former Redfearn) glassworks at Monk Bretton. In the background to the right is the Monckton coke and chemical works.

Royston station in Midland days.

Jubilee 4-6-0, 45570 *New Zealand,* **in Royston station with a possible Leeds/Sheffield stopping train. Only four coaches make up the train.** *G. Darby*

Royston shed in May 1967. The shed was situated adjacent to the station. A Stanier Black Five 4-6-0, of which Royston had a small allocation, and two 4Fs 0-6-0 are pictured outside the shed. *G. Darby*

Visiting Britannia 4-6-2, 70016 *Ariel,* **at Royston shed.** *G. Darby*

Royston shed in May 1967, six months before closure to steam. A Stanier 8F 2-8-0, 48076 awaits its next turn of duty. *G. Darby*

Another view of Royston shed in May 1967 with a Stanier 8F 2-8-0 ready to go.
G. Darby

Another one of Roystons 8Fs awaiting its next turn of duty, May 1967. *G. Darby*

Fireman Gerald Darby on the footplate of 8F 2-8-0, 48076. *G. Darby*

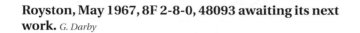

Royston, May 1967, 8F 2-8-0, 48093 awaiting its next work. *G. Darby*

Footplate crew on board 8F 2-8-0, 48093 May 1967. *G. Darby*

Stanier Black Five 4-6-0, 45079 on shed in 1966. *G. Darby*

May 1967, Britannia 4-6-2, 70046 *Anzac* **minus nameplates at Royston shed. Although barely 15/16 years old, even the Britannias were not being looked after externally.** *G. Darby*

A very atmospheric night scene of three of Royston's 8Fs at the shed entrance in 1967. *G. Darby*

Another night view of a 8F on the ashpit in 1967.
G. Darby

The last official booked steam locomotive Stanier 8F 2-8-0, 48276 on shed, 4 November 1967. The engine was booked to work the 2.35pm Royston to Goole freight returning home light engine. *G. Darby*

A view of Monk Bretton colliery in 1968. To the left of the photo is Burton Road bridge with the track and track bed of the Barnsley – Cudworth – Barnsley line. Redfearns glassworks (now Ardagh) can be seen in the background to the left. Monk Bretton station was situated at the other side of Burton Road bridge.
P. Hadfield

Another view of Monk Bretton colliery in 1968 showing Burton Road bridge and the former track and trackbed of the Barnsley – Cudworth – Barnsley line.
P. Hadfield

The Cudworth–Barnsley–Cudworth pull and push service crossing
Oaks Viaduct. The houses in the background are at Cundy Cross.
The former Barnsley coal railway can be seen in the foreground
along with the towpath of the Dearne and Dove canal. The Barnsley
canal is bridged by the viaduct at the rear of the photograph. *P. J. Lynch*

Cudworth – Barnsley – Cudworth pull and push service crossing Oaks viaduct approaching Barnsley Main colliery – Oaks Lane bridge. The engine is Ivatt class 2 2-6-2 tank 41274 and was shedded at Royston. Royston's Stanier and Ivatt tanks were extensively used on the pull and push service and the Barnsley – Sheffield – Barnsley service prior to dieselisation. *P. J. Lynch*

Stanier 2-6-2 T, 40139 crosses Oaks Viaduct with a Leeds City – Barnsley train, 24 June 1955. In the background can be seen the bridges carrying Rotherham road over the railway and the Barnsley canal (on the right). *P. J. Lynch*

Jubilee 4-6-0, 45562 *Alberta* leaves Barnsley with Saturday's only Bradford – Poole train, July/August 1966. *A.L. Brown*

Two brush type 2 diesels at Stairfoot in the early 1960s. These engines replaced steam on freight. *A. Godfrey*

The morning of 21 June 1969, the A3 Pacific 4-6-2, No. 4472 *Flying Scotsman* passes Barnsley Main and heads towards Stairfoot after stopping at the Exchange Station, Barnsley. *A.L. Brown*

On its return journey, the *Flying Scotsman* passes Barnsley Main colliery and approaches Downing's Steel Erectors. *A.L. Brown*

Preserved West Country class
4-6-2, 34092 *City of Wells*
passes through Cudworth,
1 November 1985. *P. Hadfield*

Deltic 55022 *Royal Scots Grey* passes Cudworth Station in 1991.

A diesel multiple unit being used for crew road training at Stairfoot heading towards Barnsley, 13 January 1983. *P. Hadfield*

A merry-go-round coal train passes over the road bridge at Stairfoot, once the site of Stairfoot station, 13 January 1983. The *Cross Keys Hotel* can be see on the right (now the site of McDonalds) and on the far right is the *Keel Inn*. *P. Hadfield*

Peak Class 45130 approaches Cudworth station with a Derby – York train, 9 November 1986. The author and his son, Peter, wave to the signalman G. Darby. *P. Hadfield*

Left to right, Deltics *Ballymoss*, *Pinza* and *Gordon Highlander*, stand alongside other diesel locomotives at Doncaster, 5 May 1981. *P. Hadfield*

Two EM1s pass Glasshouse crossing descending to Lewden crossing, ultimately heading to Wath marshalling yard. The rear engine is 76012. The photograph was taken on 6 July 1981. *P. Hadfield*

The Wath Banker EM1 76033 approaches at Aldham Junction, 6 July 1981. The lines to Stairfoot can be seen on the right. *P. Hadfield*

Two class 20s diesels with a train at Wath marshalling yard, 6 July 1981.
P. Hadfield

The world record holder for speed by steam traction, A4 Pacific 4-6-2 LNER 4468
Mallard **passes Wath Road junction, Manvers, with a special on 4 October 1986.**
P. Hadfield

Withdrawn Deltics at Doncaster works March 1982. The leading engine is 55015
Tulyar. *P. Hadfield*

EM1 76008 awaits cutting up at C.F. Booths Rotherham works, 9 May 1983. *P. Hadfield*

Remains of EM1s after scrapping. *P. Hadfield*

**Oaks viaduct looking towards Cundy Cross in 1968 shortly before demolition.
The area is now part of the Dearne Valley park. If this iconic structure had been
preserved it would have certainly enhanced the popularity of the park, sadly not
to be.** *A.L. Brown*

A view of the viaduct from Oaks Lane in 1968. In the background can be seen Rotherham Road, Littleworth Lane, Longcauseway estate at Monk Bretton, Redfearns glassworks (Ardagh), the terraced houses on Burton Road and the colliery spoil tip of Wharncliffe Woodmoor 4, 5 and 6 units.
A.L. Brown

This photograph is looking towards Barnsley and shows the reed-covered Dearne and Dove Canal which can be seen on the left. The canal passed under the viaduct and heads towards it's end at the Barnsley aquaduct, which carried the Barnsley canal. Barnsley Main Colliery can be seen on the left. The headgear and building is preserved as a testament to the mining industry.

Standard tank 2-6-2, 84009 rounds Barnsley Main Colliery tip heading towards Barnsley Courthouse station with the pull and push service. This engine was shedded at Royston. *P.J. Lynch*

Looking down from the Oaks viaduct at Oakwell Junction on the Barnsley coal railway a freight train heads to Stairfoot. This area is now part of the Dearne Valley park. The railway bridge over the River Dearne is now a footbridge for the public using the park. The gasometer in the background is at Old Mill, the row of houses on the far right is Castle Row at Monk Bretton, this area is now occupied by shops and housing. *P.J. Lynch*

On the Barnsley Coal Railway line a freight train passes under the near demolished Barnsley Aquaduct that once carried Barnsley canal. In the far background can be seen Bayldon Bridge, which the canal ran underneath on its way towards Cundy Cross. The aquaduct was demolished in the spring of 1954. The aquaduct abutments now carry a footbridge across the former railway and the River Dearne. This area again forms part of the Dearne Valley park. *P. Hadfield*

Underneath the aquaduct looking towards the Oaks viaduct, which can just be seen in the background under the arch. Barnsley Main Colliery can also be seen in the distance. *P. Hadfield*

A controlled explosion brings down one of the arches of the aquaduct. This view is looking towards Old Mill. The terraced houses on Burton Road can be seen through the arch on the right. *P. Hadfield*

Chapter Five

BARNSLEY EXCHANGE, COURT HOUSE STATIONS AND SHED

Barnsley Exchange

The Exchange opened on 1 July 1850 and was the first railway station serving the centre of the town. 'That disgraceful and beastly hole called a railway station,' was how it was referred to by the Town Council at the time. As time progressed the one platform station and facilities soon proved inadequate in relation to the train services using the station, and the station received further criticism. Therefore the Midland railway, not wanting to be associated with the rundown image of the Exchange station,

The platform of the Exchange station as it was in 1956. The wall of the engine shed is on the left.

A view from Jumble Lane crossing. To the right is the locomotive shed. The bus station and Court House station can be seen to the left.

A further view from
Jumble Lane crossing
showing the station
and shed.

The shed and the one platform of the Exchange
Station, as it looked during the 1950s.

A N5 tank 0-6-2, 69365 and 2 J11s 0-6-0s on shed.

progressed the building of the Court House station.

The Exchange developed a goods yard and locomotive shed, along with its one platform station, which was a delight for trainspotters as it could be viewed from the station platform and it always displayed a variety of engines. Though the smoky engines did little to improve its apprearance for the general public. One wonders what the recently crowned Queen Elizabeth II's thoughts were as she arrived at the station at three minutes to 10 on

Barnsley sheds allocation of locomotives on occasions surpassed the sheds capacity therefore engines were parked on adjacent sidings to the main line. This view is looking back towards Jumble Lane with the viaduct carrying the line to the Courthouse Station. The Ceag building is behind the viaduct and Needham and Brown factory is on the left.

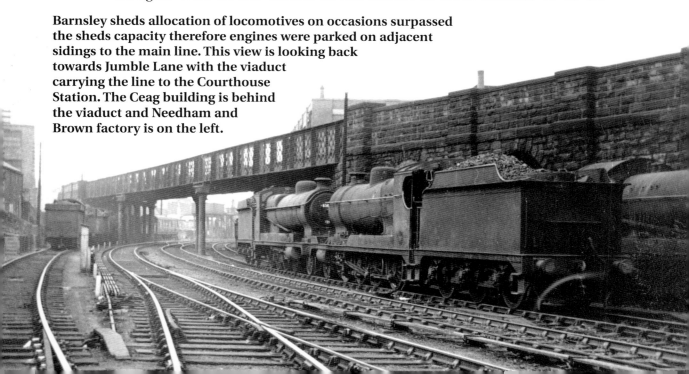

The visit of the Queen and Prince Philip to Barnsley on 27 October 1954. The Royal Train double headed by B1s 4-6-0s, 61248 *Geoffrey Gibbs* and 61250 *A Harold Bibby* passing Pindar Oaks, Measbro Dyke towards Barnsley Exchange. The four headlamps on the leading engine denotes the Royal Train.

Wednesday morning, 27 October 1954. The royal train was double-headed, being pulled by B1s 61248 *Geoffrey Gibbs* and 61250 *A Harold Bibby*.

The main purpose of the adjacent shed, like many of the sheds in our area, was to supply freight engines to transport, in the main, coal from the nearby collieries to the marshalling yards of Wath and Carlton. Stairfoot, Barnsley Main, Pinder Oaks, for example, had extensive sidings to accommodate wagons awaiting either transfer to the yards or direct to the power stations.

The upshot of this was that Barnsley shed housed engines designed for freight, i.e. O4s, J11s, C13s, C14s, N5 and austerities, even B1s were a rarity. I was taken round the shed, and will be eternally grateful to the enginemen who escorted me around, but as someone drawn to seeing A4s, A3s, A2s, A1s, V2s etc, it did not fill me with great enthusiasm. The main passenger traffic using the station was the Leeds City to Barnsley service, along with holiday excursion traffic.

Class J39 64902 at Jumble Lane crossing in May 1958. If you look to the right of the steam engine you can see the water column, which was used to take on water, a process which could take up to ten minutes. *L. Nixon*

Jubilee 4-6-0, 45643 *Rodney*, leaves Barnsley with a summer holiday train from Bradford to Weymouth, July 1966. These were the very last steam hauled regular service trains through Barnsley. The bus station, Court House station and signal box can been seen on left. To the right of the photo the former shed lines are still in situ six years after closure. *L. Nixon*

04 2-8-0, 63883 approaching Barnsley Exchange with a freight train. The coal yard to the right being owned by the Wills family. The Court House line can be seen elevated on the left of the photo. *P. Hadfield*

An Ivatt 2-6-0 engine leaves Barnsley with a passenger train heading towards Sheffield. *P.J. Lynch*

Standar 2-6-2 tank 84009 of Royston shed with the Cudworth pull and push service. The train is on the up line, indicating the engine is pushing the train to Cudworth. Oakwell Lane bridge bridging the line to the Exchange Station is shown in the background to the right. *P.J. Lynch*

Barnsley Court House station

As mentioned earlier the Court House station was built as an alternative to the Exchange Station because of the poor image the Exchange portrayed. The Midland Railway was responsible for its construction and it opened for traffic in 1870. The Old Court House building (which still stands today as a public house) was the main entrance at ground level, which was off Regent Street. After getting your ticket you climbed the stairs to enter the station, of wooden construction, a vast, aesthetic improvement on the Exchange station. This resulted in the Court House becoming the main station used for the Barnsley to Sheffield Midland, Barnsley to Sheffield Victoria, Penistone to Barnsley to Doncaster, Barnsley to Penistone and Barnsley to Cudworth services, along with holiday excursion traffic.

The selection of locomotives that could be seen during the day would be Barnsley shed's J11s (Pom Poms), C13 tanks, e.g. 67409, 67434, Royston, Leeds and Lowmoor shed's tanks, 40181, 41272, 41273, 41274,

Barnsley – Cudworth pull and push at Barnsley Court House station. The engine is 0-4-4T 1P 58075 of Royston shed.

Mexborough sheds B1 4-6-0, 61166 in Barnsley Court House station.

Mexborough, Doncaster and Immingham shed's B1s, 61165, 61166, 61167, 61250 *A Harold Bibby*, 61036 *Ralph Assheton*, 61379 *Mayflower*.

Barnsley Court House and Barnsley Exchange stations operated separately until April 1960 when, following the requirement for costly, extensive maintenance work on the viaduct adjacent to the bus station, the decision was taken by British Railways to form a junction at Quarry, by lifting the Stairfoot line and lowering the Sheffield line, therefore allowing direct access to Barnsley Exchange, which acquired a new platform on the site of the former shed. This resulted in the closure, shortly afterwards, of Court House station.

Stanier 2-6-2T, 40193 of Royston shed arrives in Court House station with a passenger train from Sheffield in 1952.

Ivatt 2-6-2T 41281. Another Royston engine in Court House station.

Two ages of steam. On the left is the C14 design of 1907 and on the right is the BR Standard class 2-6-2T of 1953. The photograph was taken in 1958.

A class 2P 4-4-0, 40512 prepares to leave Court House station in the direction of Sheffield. *Clive Pickering*

Royston sheds 1P 0-4-4T 58066 is steamed and stands on the approach to Court House station 8 June 1958. The day is a Sunday on which the Cudworth – Barnsley – Cudworth pull and push service did not run. A special had arrived at Court House station. 58066 was prepared to mark the end of the pull and push service. *Clive Pickering*

Ivatt 2-6-2 tank 41281 stands on platform 1 at Court House station. The bus station being visible on the photo as also shown on the previous page. *Clive Pickering*

The special; a three car Craven diesel unit stands on platform 2 on 8 June 1958. 58066 is seen to the left. *Clive Pickering*

Chapter Six

... AND BEYOND

Scotland Holiday – March/April 1959
My father served in the Royal Artillery regiment during the Second World War. Unfortunately, he became a prisoner of war when Singapore surrendered to the Japanese on 15 February 1942. He worked on the building of the infamous Burma to Siam 'death railway' and suffered horrendously at the hands of the Japanese, whose brutality knew no bounds. Luckily, he survived and returned home.

One of his fellow prisoner comrades was Scottish, and he lived in a small town called Markinch, near Kirkcaldy in Fife. I remember him (Jim was his

A1 4-6-2 , 60121 *Silurian* of York shed pictured in Kings Cross Station on 27 December 1961. This engine pulled us to and from Scotland on our family holiday in 1959.

A4 4-6-2, 60009 *Union of South Africa* **crossing the Forth Bridge on 1 September 1979, on route to Aberdeen. I travelled on the train starting at Edinburgh Waverley to Aberdeen and back to Edinburgh Waverley.** *P. Hadfield*

name) and his wife coming to visit us on their motorbike and sidecar. Just imagine what a journey that must have been before the advent of the motorways.

My father, mother and myself were invited to Scotland to stay with them. Thus began my first view of the splendid express passenger locomotives of the ex-LNER. We travelled initially from Barnsley Exchange to Leeds City, then caught the 'North Briton' train, being pulled by York's A1 60121 *Silurian*. I was allowed to go and see the engine, but dared not ask to go on the footplate. D49 62742 *The Braes of Derwent* was on an adjacent platform.

The journey was an experience not to be forgotten, despite being given a telling off from my mother for not paying attention to a mature lady who was trying to describe to me the various castles of the United Kingdom. I on the other hand was more interested in the engines I could spot as we passed through York, Darlington and Gateshead. Much to my delight I spotted A4, 60009 *Union of South Africa* outside Gateshead shed. On arrival at Edinburgh Waverley station, we were met by the Scottish family and we changed trains to travel to Kirkcaldy, crossing the magnificent Forth Bridge. I noticed that a Royal Navy vessel was being scrapped in the docks below. On arriving at Kirkcaldy A2, 60535 *Hornets Beauty* was standing with a train on the adjacent platform.

The holiday was thoroughly enjoyable. I have a lasting impression of the lingering smell of the nearby whisky distillery at Markinch. When the holiday was over we travelled back from Edinburgh Waverley on the *Queen of Scots* Pullman. My father was not too happy about paying extra for us to travel on the Pullman. A1, 60121 *Silurian* again hauled our train. A1, 60126 *Sir Vincent Raven* was in the station when we left, 62421 *Laird O'Monkbarns* and 62640 *Lady of the Lake* being in store in sidings outside the station. On arrival at Leeds Central we made the short journey across to City station, and finally returned by train back to Barnsley.

Doncaster 1959
Following my return from the Scottish holiday, the day that will ever stay in my mind was soon to arrive – my first visit to Doncaster. My parents only allowed me to go because there were several of us from our

Thompson B1 4-6-0, 61266, which I caught from Court House station to Doncaster on my first trip there. The engine is seen entering Stairfoot station with a passenger train. The station closed on 15 September 1957, but was still open for specials. *P. Hadfield*

Jubilee 4-6-0, 45593 *Kolhapur* leaving Doncaster on 22 April 1967 with a special being run to raise funds to buy and preserve a Jubilee loco. Ironically the choice came down to either 45562 *Alberta* or *Kolhapur*. *Kolhapur* was chosen, and runs today. *Alberta* was purchased for spares. By this date dieselisation had taken over, Doncaster shed had closed, and with it the days of spotting A4s, A3s, A2s, A1s, V2s, B1s etc had become a memory. *J. Westwood*

neighbourhood, of which some were older and would look after us during the day. Stairfoot station had closed for passengers, therefore, we had to catch the Penistone – Barnsley – Doncaster train from Barnsley Court House station. Officially the train left at 9.54am (to us it was ten to ten). Passing through Stairfoot station I wondered why it closed, when you are ten years old economics are not necessarily your strong point. The other stations on the journey, i.e. Wombwell Central, Wath Central, Mexborough and Conisbrough were all open, therefore the train stopped to pick up passengers or allow them to alight. The engine that pulled us was B1 4-6-0, 61266. (See Stairfoot section.)

On arrival at Doncaster, we stayed on the station for a short period of time. We then went to the platform near Gresley House, where cattle pens were in situ, then onto St James' Bridge and down to the shed, but we did not gain access. Afterwards we walked by the canal to the rear of the plant works to see what locomotives were on the scrap line, and we looked inside the works paint shops via a high wall.

I had never seen such a number of engines in one day as I was to experience. The sound of an A4's whistle, and everybody shouting 'streak' and the anticipation of which A4 it was going to be, was so exciting. To recount them all is beyond my memory but what I do remember was A4 60021 *Wild Swan* on the Yorkshire Pullman, A2 60500 *Edward Thompson* on the shed turntable, B1s 61001 *Eland*, 61379, *Mayflower* on shed, 60700 (the unnamed streak as we referred to it) and B17 61665 *Leicester City* on the plant scrap line. We spotted A4s (nine in total that day), A3s, A2s, A1s, V2s, B1s, B16s, K1s, K3s, O1s, O4s and austerities during the day; this will remain forever etched in my memory. The return train left Doncaster at around 5pm, and arrived back in Barnsley Court House station at around 6.10pm. I seem to think, but would stand to be corrected, that our tickets were collected at Wombwell Central station. As we passed through Stairfoot station again, I remember thinking it would have been far easier to get back home to Kendray than going through to Barnsley and then by bus to home.

This was to be the first of numerous visits to what I considered to be the Mecca of railway centres. Crewe, York, Leeds and Sheffield were good, but Doncaster will always be etched in my memory as extra special.

The train service from Penistone to Barnsley to Doncaster finished on 29 June 1959, and is still sadly lamented today.

When the train service terminated, it was the Yorkshire Traction Barnsley to Doncaster (No14) bus service that was to transport my friends and I from the bus stop at Stairfoot Co-op (now Worsbrough Motor Spares) to Doncaster via Goldthorpe; St James' Bridge or the cattle dock platform adjacent to Gresley House being the trainspotting locations. An unofficial visit to the shed and plant works (along with playing on the army tanks awaiting scrapping across from St James Bridge) would take place during

Doncaster 1959, A4 Pacific 4-6-2, 60007 *Sir Nigel Gresley* arrives in Doncaster with a special. This engine is now preserved.

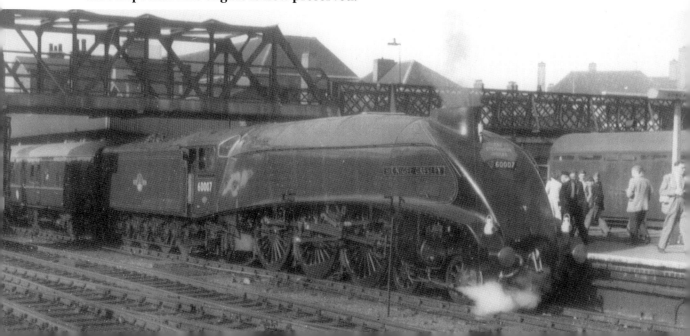

the dead hour i.e. when little traffic was passing through the station.

More often than not, the unofficial visit to the shed and works resulted in us being chased out by railway staff, although many would turn a blind eye to our presence. The plant stream of locomotives going to and from the shed and plant, comprising of locomotives going to and from overhaul, was another highlight of the day. A3, 60048 *Doncaster* springs to mind. The standby engine, in case of engine failure, was usually simmering adjacent to the goods depot and would predominantly be an A1 or V2.

During school term, we would spend Saturday at Doncaster and during the school holidays we would visit on any day of the week.

As time went by, I found I copped a very small number of locomotives previously not seen, so I would go on my bicycle on Sundays, again making

A1 Pacifics 4-6-2s, 60128 *Bongrace (below),* **60118** *Archibald Sturrock (right top),* **and 60125** *Scottish Union (right bottom),* **engines that were seen regularly at Doncaster Station and Shed.**

unofficial visits to the shed and plant works, as Sundays were quieter periods in respect of staff levels. To list the engines I saw during the Doncaster visits would be endless. There are, however, some worth recalling: the prototype blue Deltic, A4s, 60002 *Sir Murrough Wilson*, 60003 *Andrew K Macosh*, 60006 *Sir Ralph Wedgewood*, 60011 *Empire of India* (in the works), 60008 *Dwight D Eisenhower* (in the works being prepared for preservation prior to its trip to America), 60033 *Seagull* (John Lunn and myself tried to pick up its nameplate which was laying on a bench), 60022 *Mallard* on shed, 60007 *Sir Nigel Gresley* on a through express, 60025 *Falcon*, 60029 *Woodcock* on the *Flying Scotsman* and *Elizabethan* train respectively, 60027 *Merlin* on shed.

A3s, 60040 *Cameronian*, 60044 *Melton*, 60046 *Diamond Jubilee*, 60055 *Woolwinder*, 60061 *Pretty Polly*, 60103, *Flying Scotsman*, 60106 *Flying Fox*, 60109 *Hermit* (first A3 I saw fitted with the German Smoke deflectors), 60110 *Robert the Devil*.

A1s 60113 *Great Northern* (the controversial rebuild of Gresley's first Pacific), 60114 *W P Allen*, 60115 *Meg Merrilies*, 60118 *Archibald Sturrock*, 60119 *Patrick Stirling*, 60122 *Curlew*, 60123 *H A Ivatt*, 60125 *Scottish Union*, 60131 *Osprey*, 60136 *Alcazar*, 60139 *Sea Eagle*, 60144 *King's Courier*, 60149 *Amadis*, 60156 *Great Central*, 60158 *Aberdonian*.

A2s 60500 *Edward Thompson*, 60512 *Steady Aim*, 60520 *Owen Tudor*, 60521 *Watling Street*, 60523 *Sun Castle*, 60525 *A H Peppercorn*, 60533 *Happy Knight*.

V2s 60800 *Green Arrow*, 60809 *The Snapper*, 60872 *King's Own Yorkshire Light Infantry*.

B1s 61001 *Eland*, 61026 *Ourebi*, 61036 *Ralph Assheton*, 61251 *Oliver Bury*.

Britannias, 70009 *Alfred the Great* (seen at Cleethorpes) and 70035 *Rudyard Kipling*.

All unforgettable names that added to the joy of trainspotting.

I followed the progress of A3 60100 *Spearmint* on shed, in the works undergoing overhaul and in the paint shops. The Marsden rail DVD *Doncaster 1959 to 1965* shows *Spearmint* having its steam test, possibly the last major overhaul the engine underwent.

On one occasion during a visit to the scrap line, A3 60049 *Galtee More* was in the early stages of scrapping. Only its coupling/driving rods had been removed, its nameplates were still attached to the locomotive, but its smokebox number plate was laying on the ground. I picked it up, put it in my bag and then honesty foolishly got the better of me, 'What would my parents think of me, being prosecuted for trespassing and theft?' so I placed it back on the ground (still a regret today). Number plates and nameplates were being sold for a small fee or scrap value. I can verify this fact as my cousin, Ernest, a boilersmith at Ardsley and

York museum 22 April 1967, the name plates of B1, *A. Harold Bibby* and A1 *Auld Reekie* are pictured together. The engine B1 61250 was seen regularly on the Penistone – Barnsley – Doncaster service. A160160 *Auld Reekie* shedded in Scotland and was rarely seen at Doncaster. *J. Westwood*

Wakefield sheds, removed them prior to the withdrawal of a locomotive and they were packaged and sent up to York for various organisations to collect.

A visit to the Doncaster railway museum was like visiting an Aladdin's cave. A4s', A3s', A2s', A1s' B17s', D49s', Jubilees' and Royal Scots' nameplates and number plates, along with shed plates, were on view, the majority being given by the works, free of charge, and well before their value was realised in today's world of railway memorabilia.

On a sad note, my last visit in 1965 confirmed the forthcoming mass dieselisation of the system, the remaining steam locomotives looked unkempt and were in an appalling condition. It was to close the curtain on my trainspotting days.

Wath, Wath Yard, Wath Road, Manvers, Mexborough Shed and Swinton

When I was 12 years old my parents bought me a second-hand bicycle, a Raleigh Blue Streak from Wigfalls in Barnsley at a cost of £9 19s 6d, a significant amount of money for them to afford in those days. Having a bicycle opened a new world to me, I could now cycle to the railway locations which before I would reach by walking or using the bus services, which made these locations difficult or seemingly out of reach.

Wath marshalling yard had been built by the Great Central Railway, and opened in 1907. It worked on a 'hump' principle, allowing wagons to run

The last day of the Penistone – Barnsley – Doncaster service, June 1959. C14 4-4-2T 67445 stands in Wath Central station and is suitably decorated with balloons and a plaque. All traces of the station, tracks and bridge have now disappeared.

by gravity to their designated sidings. The movement of coal traffic from the surrounding coalfield was a major factor in its construction. It consisted of 110 roads, 15 reception sidings, 35 miles of track, a throughput of up to 5,000 wagons per 24 hours, and employed up to 35 men each 8 hour shift. Originally it was worked by steam in the form of six 0-8-4T, but by the time I visited the yard the system had been electrified as part of the overall Woodhead scheme.

The EMIs as seen at Swaithe were the predominant power, diesel shunters being used to prepare the trains in the yard. The best time to visit the yard was on a Sunday, as the power had been shut off and quite a large

The former Hull and Barnsley railway station at Wath. It is today a domestic residence. *P. Hadfield*

Elsecar Junction as it looked on 6 July 1981. *P. Hadfield*

number of EMIs were stabled at the shed, along with the diesel allocation. Therefore, a bike ride to Wath yard, then onto Wath Road, Manvers, and finally to Mexborough shed, proved to be a very satisfying day.

A visit to Wath today shows very little of the former importance of the dominance and heritage of the former railway system. Wath had three railway stations, Wath Central on the Barnsley to Doncaster route, Wath North on the Leeds to Sheffield Midland route and, finally the Hull and Barnsley station (station house is still intact and occupied as a domestic residence). The yard area is occupied by the Wath/Manvers road bypass and a substantial housing development, and the construction of the leisure and lake area at Manvers has obliterated the area of Wath North station. Wath Central railway station site has only been demolished in the last five years.

Wath shed and yard, 5 October 1980. *P. Hadfield*

Memorial to the Manvers – Wath train crash of 18 May 1948, erected on the crash site. *P. Hadfield*

Wath Road junction, Manvers, was an ideal spotting location, here the former Midland mainline, Leeds to Sheffield via Cudworth, was joined by the York to Sheffield (ex-Swinton and Knottingley railway) and passing underneath was the Barnsley to Doncaster line, prior to entering Mexborough. Therefore, all the expresses that had come through Cudworth (with the exception of the up Thames to Clyde and down London to Bradford), the local Leeds to Sheffield passenger trains, the freights, the York to Sheffield expresses and freights and the Barnsley to Doncaster traffic (predominantly freights with the infrequent passenger train) could be viewed.

Before moving from Wath to Mexborough, I will recall a major accident that occurred at Wath on the Midland mainline on 18 May 1948. A London St Pancras to Bradford Forster Square express, consisting of twelve coaches and double-headed by Jubilees, 5606 *Cyprus* and 5609 *Gilbert and Ellice Islands* (LMS numbers) approached Wath Road. The 18 May 1948 was a Whitsuntide Tuesday, the end of the busy holiday period, which had seen temperatures around 80 degrees Fahrenheit. The driver of the lead engine, around the

Engineering drawing of the crash site. *P. Hadfield*

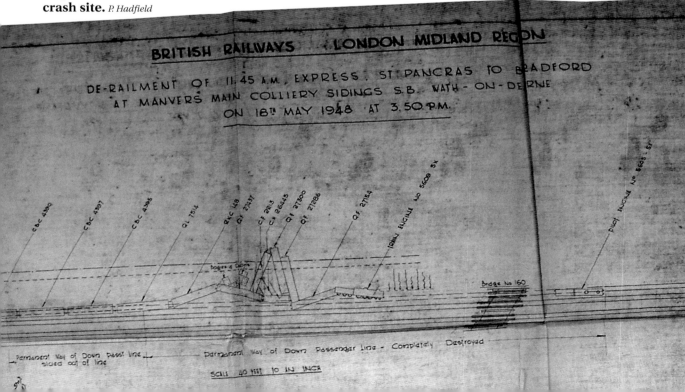

The photograph shows *Gilbert and Ellice Islands* with BR numbering i.e. 45609. This overturned at Wath on 18 May 1948. 45606 *Cyprus* remained upright.

area of Wath Road Junction, noticed a kink and distortion in the rails. Although applying the brake, it was to no avail, the train was travelling around 60mph and a resultant crash occurred. The locomotive *Cyprus* remained upright, *Gilbert and Ellice Islands* overturned, the last four coaches stayed on the rails but the first eight left the rails, overturned and concertinaed. Six passengers died initially, the driver and another passenger died later, and fifty-five passengers were admitted to Mexborough Montagu Hospital. The accident investigation concluded that the poor condition of the track and ballast (a common factor of the railways following the Second World War) had contributed to the accident. A memorial stands on the site today.

Finally, on to Mexborough shed, which had a vast array of different locomotives, predominantly a freight shed, its complement of engines mostly ranged from 04s, J11s, J69s, N5s K3s, austerities and B1s for passenger work. A visit to the shed, particularly again on a Sunday, could reveal one or two surprises, V2s and an occasional A1 or A2. The Garratt locomotive, used for banking on the Wath to Penistone route via the Worsbrough bank, had been shedded at Mexborough prior to electrification of the route and had been scrapped before my visits to the shed. As previously stated, the acquisition of a bicycle meant that I could reach places that had not realistically been possible before.

Some of my friends and I had been informed that a scrapyard in the Wath/Swinton area had received some southern region engines for scrapping. I had never seen, to date, a southern region engine, and with somewhat loose travelling directions we set off to track down the locomotives. I cannot, to this day, remember which yard it was, whether it was in Wath or Swinton, but either by pure good luck or judgment, we found the yard and the locomotives which had already been cut up but the various locomotive components, wheels, boilers, frames, coupling and driving rods, cabs, etc, had been stacked very neatly. One of the engines, I remember distinctly, was the remains of 30931 *King's Wimbledon*.

Sheffield, Hemsworth and Scarborough

My visits to Sheffield Midland were not regular because I found that predominantly the engines I saw were, in the case of expresses, engines working through to Leeds, York and beyond. Therefore the same locomotives could be seen at the Cudworth and Wath Road, Manvers' spotting locations. Although I did appreciate on occasions there would be engine changes, the retiring engines making their way to Millhouses shed. Any regret I had was that I never visited Millhouses, Grimethorpe or Darnall sheds, and Sheffield Victoria station.

Hemsworth is on the Leeds to Doncaster mainline and was within easy reach from home by bicycle. Again, I did not make regular visits as I would see the engines at Doncaster.

Scarborough Shed

While holidaying in Scarborough, I was allowed by my parents to visit the shed. The best time would be the weekend, when the holiday excursion traffic was quite heavy. My visits to the shed, unfortunately, were in midweek when the shed's locomotive stud was depleted. I did hope to see the resident D49s, but that was not to be, but to coin a phrase 'you can't win them all!'

York

Visits to York station were made by catching the train from Barnsley to Leeds, changing trains and onwards to York. York station is a magnificent structure, its architecture is first class. The beauty of trainspotting at York was that both ex-LNER and LMS engines worked to and through the station. Jubilees from Bristol, Barrow Road, Birmingham, Derby, Sheffield and Leeds sheds were regular visitors, along with Black Fives and 8Fs. A4s, A3s, A2s, A1s, V2s, B1s, B16s, D49s and K1s predominantly represented the ex-LNER types working in from the north, e.g. Edinburgh Haymarket, Heaton, Gateshead and Darlington, and from the south, Doncaster, Grantham, Peterborough, New England and King's Cross.

A particular memory that comes to mind was being allowed to cab Jubilee 45602 *British Honduras*, the fireman explaining the workings and controls of the engine. On another occasion I remember A4 60019 *Bittern* coming into the station, not in best external condition, the young fireman having difficulty opening the door on the footplate hit the door with a hammer, much to the disgust of the driver who gave him a clip round the ear and told him, in no uncertain terms, to show the engine respect. A day train spotting at York was more than worthwhile.

Leeds

Ex-LMS Jubilees, Royal Scots, 4Fs, 9Fs, Stanier and Ivatt tanks and the numerous Black Fives dominated Leeds before the advent of dieselisation in the late 1950s. Ex-LNER A3s, A1s, A2s and D49s could also be seen, along with the occasional A4; spotting 60023 *Golden Eagle* is one that springs to mind.

Leeds Holbeck's large allocation of Jubilees, for example 45562 *Alberta*, 45564 *New South Wales*, 45573 *Newfoundland*, 45675 *Hardy*, 45694 *Bellorophon*, 45708 *Resolution*, 45739 *Ulster*, Royal Scots 46145 *The Duke of Wellington Regiment* (West Riding)' and 46108 *Seaforth Highlander*. The Peaks (diesels) introduced in 1959 were starting to make a distinct impression on the expresses, such as *The Thames – Clyde Express*.

Leeds Central

One of the things I regret in life is that for some strange reason I never went trainspotting at Leeds Central. My one and only occasion when I visited the station was as a result of arriving there on the *Queen of Scots* Pullman after the Scotland holiday.

I made unofficial visits to Leeds Holbeck shed but, again, with regret did not visit Copley Hill, Neville Hill or Stourton sheds.

Crewe

As Doncaster was for me the Mecca for ex LNER engines, Crewe most definitely was the Holy Grail for ex LMS engines. My first visit to Crewe was in 1962, the journey from home consisted of bus travel to Penistone (the Barnsley to Penistone rail service had been axed previously), EM2 haulage by 27006 *Pandora* from Penistone via Woodhead through Woodhead tunnel, which was lit throughout, Longdendale, Torside, Hatfield and onwards to Manchester Piccadilly (formerly London Road), then

The tunnel at Woodhead, 1983. *P. Hadfield*

The platforms at Penistone are still used today to serve the Huddersfield services. A diesel locomotive is seen in this 1980s photograph. *P. Hadfield*

Ex-Great Central Director 4-4-0, 62666 *Zeebrugge* and a C13/14 tank double head a passenger train heading towards Penistone station in the 1950s. *P. Hadfield*

The Penistone – Barnsley – Doncaster service awaits departure with a very clean C13 4-4-2T, 67434 of Barnsley shed in 1953. *P. Hadfield*

Penistone in the 1980s. What a contrast to the above photo, the Woodhead route has closed, the weeds have blossomed on the platforms and trackbed, the sign of abandonment and desolation. *P. Hadfield*

change to another train, alighting at Crewe. The West Coast electrification was in the throes of being completed, therefore, steam still had a huge presence.

I had only seen one Coronation Pacific, 46223 *Princess Alice*; this was in Preston station. My family and I and our next door neighbours, the Cooper family, were going on holiday to Blackpool. Geoff Cooper (who was a great friend, sadly no longer with us) spotted the engine initially, showing me the engine in due course. Bear in mind, this experience was similar to seeing an A4 for the first time.

On arriving at Crewe to see Duchesses in abundance was a sight never to forget. On that first visit I remember clearly seeing 46229 *Duchess of Hamilton*, 46233 *Duchess of Sutherland* (both thankfully now preserved), 46222 *Queen Mary*, 46238 *City of Carlisle*, 46248 *City of Leeds*, *Princess Royal*, 46203 *Princess Margaret Rose* (also preserved) being hauled dead engine on shed, which could be viewed from the station's platforms, and 46208 *Princess Helena Victoria* coming into the station. Another highlight of that day was seeing my first named Western Region engine, 6953 *Leighton Hall*. I had seen pannier tanks while on holiday in Rhyl, but not a named engine. *Leighton Hall* was immaculately clean, her copper fittings enhancing her appearance.

With regard to Jubilees and Royal Scots, which were in significant numbers, I cannot recall any of them, which must be attributed to the excitement of spotting the Duchesses and Princesses for the first time. I did not arrive home until around 10.00pm. It was the first time my parents had shown any concern, which was understandable as I had got up at 6.00am that morning. Generally spotting days elsewhere would mean arriving home at 6.30 – 7.00pm. However, it was an unforgettable day, and it fuelled my appetite for further visits.

Blackpool

As a young boy growing up in the 1950s and early 1960s, family holidays were usually taken in and round Barnsley Feast week, which usually occurred in the latter part of August. The factories and mines in and around the Barnsley area closed for the week and families went by bus or train to the coast. Favourite destinations were Cleethorpes, Skegness, Mablethorpe, Great Yarmouth, Scarborough, Bridlington, Filey and Whitby on the east coast. On the west coast Blackpool was the most popular, with Rhyl, Colwyn Bay, Prestatyn and Llandudno on the north Wales coast, and Bournemouth, Torquay and Newquay on the south and south-west coast also being holiday destinations.

The Barnsley Feast week was, to the majority of families, the main holiday of the year. Working families saved up all year to pay for the week's holiday, working overtime whenever available. Apart from the working men's club trips, this would be, in the majority of cases, the only occasion to visit and enjoy the seaside. Holidays to Spain were unheard of in those days, only the rich could afford to go abroad. As a family we would holiday in Scarborough, Filey, Bridlington, Primrose Valley (caravan camp) or Blackpool, travelling either by bus or train.

Blackpool had three railway stations – North, Central (adjacent to the famous tower) and South Stations. The railway shed was situated adjacent to the Bloomfield Road ground of Blackpool FC. The shed area and tracks are now part of a substantial car and coach park. I understand that each weekend from Easter to mid-September up to sixty holiday specials went to Blackpool, packed with holidaymakers, enthralled with the prospect of having a great holiday.

I also have had a great interest in sport, in particular cricket, football and table tennis, both playing and spectating. It was during a holiday to Blackpool with my cousin, Terry, (who was a very talented footballer) and his mother, my Auntie Frances, that Terry and I went along to Blackpool FC's Bloomfield Road ground to watch the players training. It was probably 1956 or 1957. One of the star players was Ernie Taylor (later transferred to Manchester United after the Munich air disaster on 6 February 1958). Terry and I were behind the goal watching the players practising shooting at the goalkeeper. Ernie Taylor unleashed a fearsome shot which went just wide of the goal, its trajectory heading straight towards me. I turned, the ball hit me in the middle of the back, knocking me to the ground, the ball then careered into the seated area of the stand, detaching a solid metal arm rest from one of the seats. After a flood of tears I gained my composure and Ernie came up to me and apologised; he soon had me back on my feet with his words of encouragement about me playing the game. Terry later had a trial with Blackpool. They were keen to sign him, but he opted to sign for Barnsley FC instead. I accompanied him on the day of the trial and was honoured to meet the late, great Sir Stanley Matthews, who showed us around the ground. He was a man of tremendous talent, unassuming and a true gentleman.

Gaining permission from my parents to visit the shed, I would find a tremendous selection of locomotives that had carried holidaymakers from a wide area of the country, the north west, Yorkshire, Scotland and the Midlands. Locomotives that I particularly remember were Royal Scots 46168 *The Girl Guide*, 46169 *The Boy Scout*, 46170 *British Legion*, Jubilee 45584 *North West Frontier* and Black Five 45156 *Ayrshire Yeomanry*. There were countless others, which the passage of time has faded from memory.

Wakefield Shed

As previously mentioned, my cousin, Ernest, was a boilersmith based at Ardsley shed. When Copley Hill and Ardsley sheds closed, Ernest, along with the locomotives, were transferred to Wakefield shed. One Sunday morning he arranged to show me around the shed. A1 60117 *Bois Roussel*, was in steam, along with 60157 *Great Eastern,* which was at the rear of the shed. Against regulations, but to my excitement, we boarded the footplate. He released the brake and let me open the regulator; the engine moved forward a few yards at which point I closed the regulator (under his instruction) and he reapplied the brake.

We then progressed to the front of the shed to look at the engines in store, or possibly awaiting removal for scrapping. I cabbed B1 61015 *Duiker* and A1 60115 *Meg Merrilies*. In the back of my memory I seem to remember A1s 60118 *Archibald Sturrock* and 60119 *Patrick Stirling* also being in store, but I would certainly stand to be corrected. The year would be 1964/65. For the first time this made me realise that steam was really on the way out, and its days were numbered. Although there was an ever increasing dieselisation, steam was still showing a significant presence on the railway, to see A1s in store, some with only a working life of fifteen years and the list of engines being withdrawn in the monthly railway magazines, e.g. Jubilees, Royal Scots, Duchesses, A4s, A3s, A2s, A1s, V2s, B1s and, of course, the former Great Western and Southern locomotives (which I had little experience of seeing) made depressing reading for a young person still fascinated by a machine that he considered to be the closest thing to a living being.

End of an era

I was to visit Doncaster as a trainspotter for the last time in 1965. The expresses and local passenger goods trains were, predominantly, all diesel hauled. I have to admit the Deltics were a bit special, even to a steam fanatic.

The remaining steam engines on view were in an appalling state, both internally and externally. The final straw was the arrival of A1 60155 *Borderer*, of York shed, in a filthy state and leaking steam from every conceivable point. I had always admired the A1 class, their design by A. H. Peppercorn looked thoroughly modern and graceful, in my opinion. Some of the class, barely fifteen years old, with years of good service left in them, were allowed to be run down, and were operating in an appalling state. They subsequently were withdrawn and scrapped. The 9Fs, which were even younger, were dealt with in the same manner. Unfortunately this was the policy on the elimination of steam traction. Thanks to Dr Beeching.

I came away from Doncaster thinking this was a sad end for a machine that had revolutionised transport. Their service was invaluable to our country, and the world, and had given so much enjoyment and pleasure to so many, from boyhood to adolescence.

However, this was not to be the end of the story. I started work in 1965 at Wood Brothers Glass Company, situated at Hoyle Mill, Barnsley. I would walk to and from work, dependent on the weather, cross the railways adjacent to Barnsley Main Colliery (now closed), around the colliery spoil tip, or in inclement weather, down Hoyle Mill Road and Oaks Lane.

During the summer months of 1966, I became aware of a Saturdays only Bradford to Poole train, running via Barnsley, which was hauled by the surviving Jubilees based at Leeds Holbeck shed. Whenever possible, I would go to view the train on its outward and return journeys; on one occasion travelling to Sheffield Midland, and catching the train back to Barnsley. The engine was 45562 *Alberta*, which had been a regular engine on the Thames-Clyde Express and London to Bradford express, seen during my Field Lane period of trainspotting.

Other engines I remember working the Bradford to Poole train were 45581 *Bihar and Orissa*, 45593 *Kolhapur* (now preserved) and 45647

A1 4-6-2, 60155 *Borderer* as it looked when it was maintained to a decent standard.

Jubilee 4-6-0, 45562 *Alberta* stands in Barnsley station with the Saturdays only Bradford to Poole train, July/August 1966. The lines to the former shed can still be seen on the right. *A. L. Brown*

Sturdee. Along with the removal of the original nameplates, the engine nameboard had their names skilfully painted on.

On one particular occasion I was travelling by train to Sheffield, passing the former Monkspring Junction at Swaithe, when the ticket collector uttered words to the effect, 'that's the end of the Rockies.' The term 'the Rockies' was in reference to the terrain of solid sandstone that was blasted during the line's construction. We engaged in conversation and he told me he had been a fireman at Leeds Holbeck shed and during the Second World War he had experienced one of the most terrifying times of his life. He was firing a Stanier Black Five, which was in charge of a very overloaded munitions train. Leaving Cudworth and taking the Chapeltown loop over Sunny Bank viaduct, up to and through Ardsley tunnel, After coming over the viaduct at Stairfoot the line climbed steadily to Wombwell. The signal was at red at Monkspring and in the driver's opinion if they had to stop with the train vastly overloaded, as were many in wartime, there would be great difficulty in re-starting. This was a serious problem in itself, but vastly compounded by the fact that the German Luftwaffe were bombing Sheffield. The signal did not change, despite the Black Five's whistle working overtime. The train had to stop, and was completely exposed to the returning German bombers. Fortunately, the train was not attacked, a locomotive was dispatched to help re-start the train and, to add insult to injury, the stop signal was to allow the passage of the Barnsley to Sheffield, two coach pull and push service.

During the summer months of 1967, when colleges and universities closed for the summer recess, Woods Brothers employed students, usually known to the Woods' family. I worked in the laboratory and we usually had a university student placed to work with us. One such student was a gentleman called John Westwood, who was studying at Oxford University, a good cricketer and a keen railway enthusiast. He was aware of a special train going through Doncaster to raise funds to preserve a Jubilee Class engine. The special was hauled by Jubilee 45593 *Kolhapur* (now preserved). From Doncaster we caught the train to York, and went around the shed, which was still open, to find A4 60019 *Bittern* in the shed, thankfully bought

A4 4-6-2, 60019 *Bittern* , bought for preservation in York shed, 22 April 1967.
J. Westwood

Standard 2-6-0, 77012 only introduced in 1954, nearing the end of a very short working life alongside a K1 in York shed, 22 April 1967. *J.Westwood*

by a Mr G. Drury to be preserved. Active locomotives in the shed (now the National Railway Museum) consisted of K1s, BR standards and B1s, most notably minus nameplates, 61189 *Sir William Gray*. We travelled from York to Leeds, where one of the surviving Jubilees 45647 *Sturdee* was on view, and finally on to Keighley. Stanier Black Fives were still making a notable presence through the station. We progressed to Haworth on the Keighley and Worth Valley railway to view Royal Scot 46115 *Scots Guardsman*, again thankfully purchased for preservation.

Locally, steam was still making a showing through Stairfoot in 1967. Royston shed stayed open to steam until 4 November 1967 and her remaining 8Fs could be seen and heard transporting, in the main, 'black diamonds' (coal) from Carlton yard to Wath yard and vice versa. Officially, the last booked engine was 8F 48276 working to and from Goole, but I am

B1 4-6-0, 61189 *Sir William Gray* **shorn of name plates stands in York shed 22 April 1967.** *J.Westwood*

K1 2-6-0 stands in York shed, 22 April 1967. The shed and buildings now form part of the National Railway Museum. *J.Westwood*

Royal Scot 4-6-0, 46115 *Scots Guardsman* **at Haworth on the Keighley and Worth railway. Thankfully the engine had been bought for preservation.** *J. Westwood*

The engine is being cleaned and the author is facing the camera. *J. Westwood*

reliably informed that 8Fs 48222 and 48169 later came on shed.

Royston's 8Fs played out the final swansong of steam in the area. Brush Type 2 diesels, diesel shunters and English Electric Type 3s then undertook steam's former duties.

Steam finished on British Railways on 10 August 1968. To me it was the end of an era. However probably the most famous locomotive – certainly in the United Kingdom – LNER A3 Pacific 4472 (BR no 60103) *Flying Scotsman*, still had running powers over British Railways' metals. It was to pass through Barnsley and Stairfoot on 21 June 1969. I photographed her

21 June 1969, LNER Pacific 4-6-2, 4472 *Flying Scotsman* **passes through Stairfoot.** *P. Hadfield*

School children gathered around the *Flying Scotsman* as it arrived at the Exchange station in June 1969 for a two minute stop on its way to Cleethorpes. It arrived again in the evening at 9.09p.m. Below is the report from the *Barnsley Chronicle*.

y, June 28, 1969.

'Flying Scotsman' arrives — 18 minutes late

The era of the steam locomotive re-opened in Barnsley on Saturday with a proud visit of the "Flying Scotsman". It arrived amid cheers on two occasions during the day—and thrilled both young and old.

The scenes, both morning and evening, were reminiscent of Barnsley Feast Saturday, with a crowded platform awaiting the Blackpool special.

Mums and dads took along the family for the short free gaze at a monster of the track which was saved from the scrapyard.

As the loco hissed its way along the platform the youngsters were caught up with one of the most romantic forms of transport—the steam engine.

For many of the youngsters i⁺ was their first glimpse of steam locomotion.

Every bridge, street end and road near the rail track on which the "Flying Scotsman" travelled, had groups of waving admirers.

They had the Barnsley Chronicle to thank. For only an exclusive story in last week's edition notified them of the loco's visit.

Like the famous engine, this proved the "pulling power" of the Chronicle.

About a thousand people gathered in bright sunshine to see the engine's arrival in the morning.

It was 18 minutes late, but it did not dampen the enthusiasm of onlookers who thronged the platform, bridge and every available vantage point.

A two-minute stop, and,

with a wave from the crew, the engine was on its way to Cleethorpes.

The evening visit was smack on time — 9.9 p.m. The train stopped for a few minutes and the crowds then dashed to the northern end of the platform to get a closer view.

Some climbed up to the driver's cab, some wrote their names on the dusty tender, others just looked in amazement.

Happy memories for many! Everyone but the "Flying Scotsman", for on its way out of town it came to an unexpected halt near the Huddersfield-road bridge. It could not get up the incline—until assistance was given by a banker.

Such things happen—even to the greatest!

HUNDREDS OF CHIL Saturday.

coming through Stairfoot in the morning, and watched her return in the evening. The lineside was packed with people of all ages.

The Dearne Valley railway

The DVR ran through Ryhill, Shafton, Grimethorpe, Houghton, Thurnscoe, Goldthorpe, Harlington, Denaby to Edlington. The passenger service from Wakefield was terminated in September 1951 long before my spotting days, therefore freight (mainly coal) was the predominant traffic. I understand the stations were very sparse affairs. I never visited the line to trainspot. A connecting curve was constructed from the mainline south of Cudworth through to Grimethorpe and Houghton in 1966, resulting in the majority of the line being redundant. However, the magnificient Dearne Valley viaduct across the River Don at Conisborough is a reminder of the line's former glory.

GALA DAY SPECIAL

her round the world-famous "Flying Scotsman" as it pulls into Barnsley railway station on

Chapter Seven

CONCLUSION

THERE, SO I thought ended an unforgettable chapter of my life, the memories still stirring my imagination at various times. Virtually every boy of my generation, at some stage, spent time trainspotting, it was part of our lives.

When the ban on steam on the main line was lifted the preservation societies gathered momentum, not in any small way due to the acquisition of locomotives from Dai Woodham's yard at Barry Docks (to which I made the pilgrimage), and subsequent restoration. I visited the railway preservation centres and took trips periodically on the steam hauled tours, e.g. over the settle and Carlisle line and East Coast main line.

A good friend, Gerald Darby, formerly a fireman at Royston shed and later a signalman at Cudworth and Barnsley, would inform me of any specials or locomotives passing through Cudworth, Barnsley or Wath, and I would photograph them whenever possible. With the closure of the Woodhead route and Wath yard I photographed the EMIs in their last days,

West Country Pacific 4-6-2, 34070 *Manston* at Barry docks August 1979 purchased for preservation. The author is stood by the locomotive. *P. Hadfield*

Barry docks in 1978. Jubilee 4-6-0, 45699 *Galatea* with the author on the footplate. The engine is now preserved and running on the main line. *P. Hadfield*

watched them being scrapped at C.F. Booth's yard in Rotherham, along with the later scrapping of the Advanced Passenger Train.

I also photographed the Deltics, which I had seen since their introduction, their working and subsequent withdrawal and storage at Doncaster plant works.

Much of the railway system in the Barnsley area, as in so many other locations, has disappeared. However, some of the trackbeds have been made into walkways, bridle paths and extensively incorporated into sections of the Trans-Pennine trail, e.g. Woodhead Route, Barnsley to Wath. It is hard for any youngster dining at McDonalds at Stairfoot to imagine that this was the site of Stairfoot station, and the adjacent cycle path/walkway was the trackbed, such has been the rapid changes that have taken place on our former railway system. As the 'sands of time' drew the curtain down on my sporting days of playing cricket, football and table tennis, my interest in keeping active turned to cycling. Today, as I cycle along the various sections of former railway trackbeds which have now become part of the Trans-Pennine Trail, the memories stir in my mind of the time when the railway system was in full use and, finally, at places identifying the remains of a bygone age.

However, it is not all negative, the Leeds to Barnsley to Sheffield and the

On 5 May 1981, the company I worked for had the waste management contract for Doncaster plant works, therefore I could visit the works on a regular basis. Here I am stood alongside Deltic 55007 *Pinza*. If steam had still been king, I may have applied for my office to be based at the works. *P. Hadfield*

Sheffield to Huddersfield services via Barnsley and Penistone thrive, the building and opening of the Meadowhall shopping centre has helped increase levels of passengers using the service. The new Barnsley Interchange is a vast improvement on the old station. The former Midland main line from Leeds to Sheffield via Cudworth terminates before Cudworth and is used as a freight line, serving the Ardagh Glass factory (formerly Redfearns). Surely the proposed route of HS2 could incorporate predominantly the existing trackbed of the Midland Mainline from Sheffield to Leeds, making a huge financial saving on the project. Fund-raising is taking place to extend the Elsecar branch from the Elsecar Heritage Centre to the Cortonwood shopping centre.

I have included a large selection of photographs in this book and I

EM1s awaiting scrapping at C.F. Booths at Rotherham works, 9 May 1983.
P. Hadfield

sincerely hope that readers enjoy the contents. I am sure it will stir their own memories of a magical time in railway history.

The advanced passenger train (APT) a project not carried to finalisation by British rail despite considerable investment awaits scrapping at C.F. Booths, Rotherham Works, on 8 July 1986. *P. Hadfield*

Barry docks, 9 October 1980. Battle of Britain class 4-6-2, 34072 *257 Squadron* awaits removal for preservation. Ex-GWR4612, ex-LMS 42859 and Merchant Navy 35027 *Portline* can be seen in the background. *P. Hadfield*

The remains of EM1 76014 following cutting up at C.F. Booths Rotherham works, 9 May 1983. *P. Hadfield*

"Jubilee" Class

4-6-0 **6P5F & 7P**

6P5F. Introduced 1934. Stanier L.M.S. taper boiler development of the "Patriot" class.

†Fitted with double chimney.

*7P. Introduced 1942. Rebuilt with larger boiler and double chimney.

Weight: Loco. { 79 tons 11 cwt. / 82 tons 0 cwt.*

Pressure: { 225 lb. Su. / 250 lb. Su.

Cyls.: (3) 17" × 26".

Driving Wheels: 6' 9".

T.E.: { 26,610 lb. / 29,570 lb.*

Walschaerts valve gear. P.V.

45552	Silver Jubilee
45553	Canada
45554	Ontario
45555	Quebec
45556	Nova Scotia
45557	New Brunswick
45558	Manitoba
45559	British Columbia
45560	Prince Edward Island
45561	Saskatchewan
45562	Alberta
45563	Australia
45564	New South Wales
45565	Victoria
45566	Queensland
45567	South Australia
45568	Western Australia
45569	Tasmania
45570	New Zealand
45571	South Africa
45572	Eire
45573	Newfoundland
45574	India
45575	Madras
45576	Bombay
45577	Bengal
45578	United Provinces
45579	Punjab
45580	Burma
45581	Bihar and Orissa
45582	Central Provinces
45583	Assam
45584	North West Frontier
45585	Hyderabad
45586	Mysore
45587	Baroda
45588	Kashmir
45589	Gwalior
45590	Travancore
45591	Udaipur
45592	Indore
45593	Kolhapur
45594	Bhopal
45595	Southern Rhodesia
45596†	Bahamas
45597	Barbados
45598	Basutoland
45599	Bechuanaland
45600	Bermuda
45601	British Guiana
45602	British Honduras
45603	Solomon Islands
45604	Ceylon
45605	Cyprus
45606	Falkland Islands
45607	Fiji
45608	Gibraltar
45610	Ghana
45611	Hong Kong
45612	Jamaica
45613	Kenya
45614	Leeward Islands
45615	Malay States
45617	Mauritius
45618	New Hebrides
45620	North Borneo
45621	Northern Rhodesia
45622	Nyasaland
45623	Palestine
45624	St. Helena
45625	Sarawak
45626	Seychelles
45627	Sierra Leone
45628	Somaliland
45629	Straits Settlements
45630*	Swaziland
45631	Tanganyika
45632	Tonga
45633	Aden
45634	Trinidad
45635	Tobago
45636	Uganda
45638	Zanzibar
45639	Raleigh
45640	Frobisher
45641	Sandwich
45642	Boscawen
45643	Rodney
45644	Howe
45645	Collingwood
45646	Napier
45647	Sturdee
45648	Wemyss
45649	Hawkins
45650	Blake
45651	Shovell
45652	Hawke
45653	Barham
45654	Hood
45655	Keith
45656	Cochrane
45657	Tyrwhitt
45658	Keyes
45659	Drake
45660	Rooke
45661	Vernon
45662	Kempenfelt
45663	Jervis
45664	Nelson
45665	Lord Rutherford of Nelson
45666	Cornwallis
45667	Jellicoe
45668	Madden
45669	Fisher
45670	Howard of Effingham
45671	Prince Rupert
45672	Anson
45673	Keppel
45674	Duncan
45675	Hardy
45676	Codrington
45677	Beatty
45678	De Robeck
45679	Armada
45680	Camperdown
45681	Aboukir
45682	Trafalgar
45683	Hogue
45684	Jutland
45685	Barfleur
45686	St. Vincent
45687	Neptune
45688	Polyphemus
45689	Ajax
45690	Leander
45691	Orion
45692	Cyclops
45693	Agamemnon
45694	Bellerophon
45695	Minotaur
45696	Arethusa
45697	Achilles
45698	Mars
45699	Galatea
45700	Amethyst
45701	Conqueror
45702	Colossus
45703	Thunderer
45704	Leviathan
45705	Seahorse
45706	Express
45707	Valiant
45708	Resolution
45709	Implacable
45710	Irresistible
45711	Courageous
45712	Victory
45713	Renown
45714	Revenge
45715	Invincible
45716	Swiftsure
45717	Dauntless
45718	Dreadnought
45719	Glorious
45720	Indomitable
45721	Impregnable
45722	Defence

66

67

The following pages contain extracts from my 1962 combined volume. I did not see them all but what I did see remain etched in my mind forever, confirming a magical time in my life.

45723	Fearless
45724	Warspite
45725	Repulse
45726	Vindictive
45727	Inflexible
45728	Defiance
45729	Furious
45730	Ocean
45731	Perseverance
45732	Sanspareil
45733	Novelty
45734	Meteor
45735*	Comet
45736*	Phoenix
45737	Atlas
45738	Samson
45739	Ulster
45740	Munster
45741	Leinster
45742	Connaught

Total 187

"Royal Scot" Class

4-6-0   **7P**

Introduced 1943. Stanier rebuild of Fowler L.M.S. locos. (introduced 1927) with taper boiler, new cylinders and double chimney.

*Introduced 1935. Stanier taper boiler rebuild with simple cylinders of experimental high pressure compound loco. No. 6399 Fury. (Introduced 1929.)

Weight: Loco. {83 tons. / 84 tons 1 cwt.*
Pressure: 250 lb. Su.
Cyls.: (3) 18" × 26".
Driving Wheels: 6' 9".
T.E.: 33,150 lb.
Walschaerts valve gear. P.V.

46100	Royal Scot
46101	Royal Scots Grey
46102	Black Watch
46103	Royal Scots Fusilier
46104	Scottish Borderer
46105	Cameron Highlander
46106	Gordon Highlander
46107	Argyll and Sutherland Highlander
46108	Seaforth Highlander
46109	Royal Engineer
46110	Grenadier Guardsman
46111	Royal Fusilier
46112	Sherwood Forester
46113	Cameronian
46114	Coldstream Guardsman
46115	Scots Guardsman
46116	Irish Guardsman
46117	Welsh Guardsman
46118	Royal Welch Fusilier
46119	Lancashire Fusilier
46120	Royal Inniskilling Fusilier
46121	Highland Light Infantry, City of Glasgow Regiment
46122	Royal Ulster Rifleman
46123	Royal Irish Fusilier
46124	London Scottish
46125	3rd Carabinier
46126	Royal Army Service Corps
46127	Old Contemptibles
46128	The Lovat Scouts
46129	The Scottish Horse
46130	The West Yorkshire Regiment
46131	The Royal Warwickshire Regiment
46132	The King's Regiment Liverpool
46133	The Green Howards
46134	The Cheshire Regiment
46135	The East Lancashire Regiment
46136	The Border Regiment
46137	The Prince of Wales's Volunteers (South Lancashire)
46138	The London Irish Rifleman
46139	The Welch Regiment

46140	The King's Royal Rifle Corps
46141	The North Staffordshire Regiment
46142	The York & Lancaster Regiment
46143	The South Staffordshire Regiment
46144	Honourable Artillery Company
46145	The Duke of Wellington's Regt. (West Riding)
46146	The Rifle Brigade
46147	The Northamptonshire Regiment
46148	The Manchester Regiment
46149	The Middlesex Regiment
46150	The Life Guardsman
46151	The Royal Horse Guardsman
46152	The King's Dragoon Guardsman
46153	The Royal Dragoon
46154	The Hussar
46155	The Lancer
46156	The South Wales Borderer
46157	The Royal Artilleryman
46158	The Loyal Regiment
46159	The Royal Air Force
46160	Queen Victoria's Rifleman
46161	King's Own
46162	Queen's Westminster Rifleman
46163	Civil Service Rifleman
46164	The Artists' Rifleman
46165	The Ranger (12th London Regt.)
46166	London Rifle Brigade
46167	The Hertfordshire Regiment
46168	The Girl Guide
46169	The Boy Scout
46170*	British Legion

Total 71

"Princess" Class

4-6-2   **8P**

*Introduced 1933. Stanier L.M.S. taper boiler design.
Remainder. Introduced 1935. Development of original design with alterations to valve gear, boiler and other details.

Weight. Loco. 104 tons 10 cwt.
Pressure: 250 lb. Su.
Cyls.: (4) 16¼" × 28".
Driving Wheels: 6' 6".
T.E.: 40,285 lb.

Walschaerts valve gear (inside valves operated by rocking shafts on No. 46205, remainder have four sets of valve gear). P.V.

46200*	The Princess Royal
46201*	Princess Elizabeth
46203	Princess Margaret Rose
46204	Princess Louise
46205	Princess Victoria
46206	Princess Marie Louise
46207	Princess Arthur of Connaught
46208	Princess Helena Victoria
46209	Princess Beatrice
46210	Lady Patricia
46211	Queen Maud
46212	Duchess of Kent

Total 12

"Coronation" Class

4-6-2   **8P**

Introduced 1937. Stanier L.M.S. enlargement of "Princess Royal" class. All except Nos. 46230-4/49-55 originally streamlined. (Streamlining removed from 1946.)
*Introduced 1947. Ivatt development with roller bearings and detail alterations.

NUMERICAL LIST OF ENGINES

The code given in smaller bold type at the head of each class, e.g. "4MT", denotes its British Railways power classification.
The numbers of locomotives in service have been checked in E. & N.E.R. to September 2nd, 1961, L.M.R. to August 12th, 1961, and Sc.R. to August 26th, 1961.

Class A4

4-6-2   **8P6F**

Introduced 1935. Gresley streamlined design with corridor tender (except those marked †). All fitted with double chimney.
*Inside cylinder reduced to 17".
Weight: Loco. 102 tons 19 cwt.
Tender {64 tons 19 cwt. / 60 tons 7 cwt.†
Pressure: 250 lb. Su.
Cyls.: {(3) 18½" × 26". / (2) 18½" × 26" (1) 17" × 26".*
Driving Wheels: 6' 8"
T.E.: {35,455 lb. / 33,616 lb.*
Walschaerts valve gear and derived motion. P.V.

60001†	Sir Ronald Matthews
60002†	Sir Murrough Wilson
60003†	Andrew K. McCosh
60004	William Whitelaw
60005†	Sir Charles Newton
60006†	Sir Ralph Wedgwood
60007	Sir Nigel Gresley
60008†	Dwight D. Eisenhower
60009	Union of South Africa
60010	Dominion of Canada
60011	Empire of India
60012*	Commonwealth of Australia
60013	Dominion of New Zealand
60014	Silver Link
60015	Quicksilver
60016†	Silver King
60017	Silver Fox
60018†	Sparrow Hawk
60019†	Bittern
60020*†	Guillemot
60021	Wild Swan
60022	Mallard
60023†	Golden Eagle
60024	Kingfisher
60025	Falcon
60026†	Miles Beevor
60027	Merlin
60028	Walter K. Whigham
60029	Woodcock
60030	Golden Fleece
60031	Golden Plover
60032	Gannet
60033	Seagull
60034	Lord Faringdon

Total 34

Class A3

4-6-2   **7P6F**

Introduced 1927. Development of Gresley G.N. 180 lb. Pacific (introduced 1922, L.N.E.R. A1, later A10) with 220 lb. pressure (prototype and others rebuilt from A10). Some have G.N.-type tender with coal rails†, remainder L.N.E.R. pattern. All fitted with double chimney.
Weight: Loco. 96 tons 5 cwt.
Tender {56 tons 6 cwt.† / 57 tons 18 cwt.
Pressure: 220 lb. Su.
Cyls.: (3) 19" × 26".
Driving Wheels: 6' 8".
T.E.: 32,910 lb.
Walschaerts valve gear and derived motion. P.V.

60035	Windsor Lad
60036	Colombo
60037	Hyperion
60038	Firdaussi

60039	Sandwich
60040	Cameronian
60041	Salmon Trout
60042	Singapore
60043	Brown Jack
60044	Melton
60045	Lemberg
60046	Diamond Jubilee
60047	Donovan
60048	Doncaster
60049	Galtee More
60050	Persimmon
60051	Blink Bonny
60052	Prince Palatine
60053	Sansovino
60054	Prince of Wales
60055	Woolwinder
60056	Centenary
60057	Ormonde
60058	Blair Athol
60059	Tracery
60060	The Tetrarch
60061	Pretty Polly
60062	Minoru
60063	Isinglass
60064	Tagalie
60065	Knight of Thistle
60066	Merry Hampton
60067	Ladas
60068	Sir Visto
60069	Sceptre
60070	Gladiateur
60071	Tranquil
60072	Sunstar
60073	St. Gatien
60074	Harvester
60075	St. Frusquin
60076	Galopin
60077	The White Knight
60078	Night Hawk
60079	Bayardo
60080	Dick Turpin
60081	Shotover
60082	Neil Gow
60083	Sir Hugo
60084	Trigo
60085	Manna
60086	Gainsborough
60087	Blenheim
60088	Book Law
60089	Felstead
60090	Grand Parade
60091	Captain Cuttle
60092	Fairway
60093	Coronach
60094	Colorado
60096	Papyrus
60097	Humorist
60098	Spion Kop
60099	Call Boy
60100	Spearmint
60101	Cicero
60102	Sir Frederick Banbury
60103	Flying Scotsman
60105	Victor Wild
60106	Flying Fox
60107	Royal Lancer
60108	Gay Crusader
60109	Hermit
60110	Robert the Devil
60111	Enterprise
60112	St. Simon

Total 76

Class A1

4-6-2   **8P6F**

A1/1   Introduced 1945. Thompson rebuild of A10.
A1   Peppercorn development of A1/1 for new construction.
A1†   Fitted with roller bearings.
Weight: Loco. {101 tons. / 104 tons 2 cwt.
Tender 60 tons 7 cwt.
Pressure: 250 lb. Su.
Cyls.: (3) 19" × 26".
Driving Wheels: 6' 8".
T.E.: 37,400 lb.
Walschaerts valve gear. P.V.

60113*	Great Northern
60114	W. P. Allen
60115	Meg Merrilies
60116	Hal o' the Wynd

60117-60535

60117	Bois Roussel
60118	Archibald Sturrock
60119	Patrick Stirling
60120	Kittiwake
60121	Silurian
60122	Curlew
60123	H. A. Ivatt
60124	Kenilworth
60125	Scottish Union
60126	Sir Vincent Raven
60127	Wilson Worsdell
60128	Bongrace
60129	Guy Mannering
60130	Kestrel
60131	Osprey
60132	Marmion
60133	Pommern
60134	Foxhunter
60135	Madge Wildfire
60136	Alcazar
60137	Redgauntlet
60138	Boswell
60139	Sea Eagle
60140	Balmoral
60141	Abbotsford
60142	Edward Fletcher
60143	Sir Walter Scott
60144	King's Courier
60145	Saint Mungo
60146	Peregrine
60147	North Eastern
60148	Aboyeur
60149	Amadis
60150	Willbrook
60151	Midlothian
60152	Holyrood
60153†	Flamboyant
60154†	Bon Accord
60155†	Borderer
60156†	Great Central
60157†	Great Eastern
60158	Aberdonian
60159	Bonnie Dundee
60160	Auld Reekie
60161	North British
60162	Saint Johnstoun

Total 50

102

4-6-2   8P7F   Class A2

A2/3 Introduced 1946. Development of Thompson Class A2/2 for new construction.
Weight: Loco. 101 tons 10 cwt.
Pressure: 250 lb. Su.
Cyls.: (3) 19" × 26".
Driving Wheels: 6' 2".
T.E.: 40,430 lb.

A2* Introduced 1947. Peppercorn development of Class A2/2 with shorter wheelbase. (No. 60539 built with double chimney.)

A2† Rebuilt with double chimney and multiple valve regulator.
Weight: Loco. 101 tons.
Pressure: 250 lb. Su.
Cyls.: (3) 19" × 26".
Driving Wheels: 6' 2".
T.E.: 40,430 lb.
Tender weight (all parts): 60 tons 7 cwt.
Walschaerts valve gear. P.V.

60500	Edward Thompson
60511	Airborne
60512	Steady Aim
60513	Dante
60514	Chamossaire
60515	Sun Stream
60516	Hycilla
60517	Ocean Swell
60518	Tehran
60519	Honeyway
60520	Owen Tudor
60521	Watling Street
60522	Straight Deal
60523	Sun Castle
60524	Herringbone
60525*	A. H. Peppercorn
60526†	Sugar Palm
60527*	Sun Chariot
60528*	Tudor Minstrel
60529†	Pearl Diver
60530*	Sayajirao
60531*	Bahram
60532†	Blue Peter
60533†	Happy Knight
60534*	Irish Elegance
60535*	Hornet's Beauty

60536-60869

60536*	Trimbush
60537*	Bachelor's Button
60538†	Velocity
60539*	Bronzino

Total
Class A2   15   Class A2/3 15

2-6-2   7P6F   Class V2

Introduced 1936. Gresley design.
*Fitted with double chimney.
Weight: Loco. 93 tons 2 cwt. Tender 52 tons.
Pressure: 220 lb. Su.
Cyls.: (3) 18½" × 26".
Driving Wheels: 6' 2".
T.E.: 33,730 lb.
Walschaerts valve gear and derived motion. P.V.

60800	Green Arrow
60801	
60802	
60803	
60804	
60805	
60806	
60807	
60808	
60809	The Snapper. The East Yorkshire Regiment. The Duke of York's Own
60810	
60811	
60812	
60813	
60814	
60815	
60816	
60817*	
60818	
60819	
60820	
60821	
60822	
60823	
60824	
60825	
60826	
60827	
60828	
60829	
60830	
60831	
60832	
60833	
60834	
60835	The Green Howard, Alexandra, Princess of Wales's Own Yorkshire Regiment
60836	
60837	
60838	
60839	
60840	
60841	
60842	
60843	
60844	
60845	
60846	
60847	St. Peter's School York A.D. 627
60848	
60849	
60850	
60851	
60852	
60853	
60854	
60855	
60856	
60857	
60858	
60859	
60860	Durham School
60861	
60862	
60863	
60864	
60865	
60866	
60867	
60868	
60869	

103

60870-61065

60870
60871
60872 King's Own Yorkshire Light Infantry
60873 Coldstreamer
60874

60875	60897	60919	60941
60876	60898	60920	60942
60877	60899	60921	60943
60878	60900	60922	60944
60879	60901	60923	60945
60880	60902	60924	60946
60881*	60903	60925	60947
60882	60904	60926	60948
60883	60905	60927	60949
60884	60906	60928	60950
60885	60907	60929	60951
60886	60908	60930	60952
60887	60909	60931	60953
60888	60910	60932	60954
60889	60911	60933	60955
60890	60912	60934	60956
60891	60913	60935	60957
60892	60914	60936	60958
60893	60915	60937	60959
60894	60916	60938	60960
60895	60917	60939	60961
60896	60918	60940	60962

60963*
60964 The Durham Light Infantry

60965	60970	60975	60980
60966	60971	60976	60981
60967	60972	60977	60982
60968	60973	60978	60983
60969	60974	60979	

Total 184

61000 Springbok
61001 Eland
61002 Impala
61003 Gazelle
61004 Oryx
61005 Bongo
61006 Blackbuck
61007 Klipspringer
61008 Kudu
61009 Hartebeeste
61010 Wildebeeste
61011 Waterbuck
61012 Puku
61013 Topi
61014 Oribi
61015 Duiker
61016 Inyala
61017 Bushbuck
61018 Gnu
61019 Nilghai
61020 Gemsbok
61021 Reitbok
61022 Sassaby
61023 Hirola
61024 Addax
61025 Pallah
61026 Ourebi
61027 Madoqua
61028 Umseke
61029 Chamois
61030 Nyala
61031 Reedbuck
61032 Stembok
61033 Dibatag
61034 Chiru
61035 Pronghorn
61036 Ralph Assheton
61037 Jairou
61038 Blacktail
61039 Steinbok
61040 Roedeer

61041	61047	61053	61060
61042	61048	61054	61061
61043	61049	61055	61062
61044	61050	61056	61063
61045	61051	61058	61064
61046	61052	61059	61065

4-6-0 5MT **Class B1**

Introduced 1942. Thompson design.
Weight: Loco. 71 tons 3 cwt.
Tender 52 tons.
Pressure: 225 lb. Su.
Cyls.: (O) 20" x 26".
Driving Wheels: 6' 2".
T.E.: 26,880 lb.
Walschaerts valve gear. P.V

61066-61251

61066	61097	61128	61159	61205
61067	61098	61129	61160	61206
61068	61099	61130	61161	61207
61069	61100	61131	61162	61208
61070	61101	61132	61163	61209
61071	61102	61133	61164	61210
61072	61103	61134	61165	61211
61073	61104	61135	61166	61212
61074	61105	61136	61167	61213
61075	61106	61137	61168	61214
61076	61107	61138	61169	61215 William Henton Carver
61077	61108	61139	61170	61216
61078	61109	61140	61171	61217
61079	61110	61141	61172	61218
61080	61111	61142	61173	61219
61081	61112	61143	61174	61220
61082	61113	61144	61175	61221 Sir Alexander Erskine-Hill
61083	61114	61145	61176	61222
61084	61115	61146	61177	61223
61085	61116	61147	61178	61224
61086	61117	61148	61179	61225
61087	61118	61149	61180	61226
61088	61119	61150	61181	61227
61089	61120	61151	61182	61228
61090	61121	61152	61183	61229
61091	61122	61153	61184	61230
61092	61123	61154	61185	61231
61093	61124	61155	61186	61232
61094	61125	61156	61187	61233
61095	61126	61157	61188	61234
61096	61127	61158		61235

61189 Sir William Gray
61190
61191
61192
61193
61194
61195
61196
61197
61198
61199
61200
61201
61202
61203
61204

61236
61237 Geoffrey H. Kitson
61238 Leslie Runciman
61239
61240 Harry Hinchcliffe
61241 Viscount Ridley
61242 Alexander Reith Gray
61243 Sir Harold Mitchell
61244 Strang Steel
61245 Murray of Elibank
61246 Lord Balfour of Burle...
61247 Lord Burghley
61248 Geoffrey Gibbs
61249 FitzHerbert Wright
61250 A. Harold Bibby
61251 Oliver Bury